Endorsements

"I have known Ruth for about 10 years and have had the privilege of [   ] wisdom, knowledge and practical tools to lead in a more intentional, thoughtful and productive manner. By nature Ruth is a mentor. She teaches, not lectures, and empowers others to learn to think through the challenges finding solutions and ultimately helping leaders achieve greater impact in the lives of those they lead. Ruth has taught me to remove myself from the immediate... from the daily crises and get to higher ground for perspective and ways to lead through the fray to the calm.

Thanks Ruth, for always listening and driving to helpful understanding in difficult workplace challenges. And thanks for seeing potential that I didn't see."

Heather Wile
Communications Director
First Alliance Church, Calgary Alberta

"Ruth is a stellar encourager. She came into my life when I felt I was at the lowest of leadership ability. She always inspires me to dig a little deeper in my leadership skills. She is a wonderful listener and catches nuances of conversations which lead to a word of wisdom in her interaction in our conversations. Ruth asks lots of questions that really make me pause to consider my stance on any given situation. This has helped me to consider asking myself similar questions as I mull over situations before me. Her ability to spur on thoughts in another direction using questions like, "I wonder what it would look like if we thought about this ...?" She has a unique way of looking at situations from a different perspective than mine, which has enabled me in making leadership decisions. I love her position of seeking wisdom around the table and her own aha moments during any discussion or conversations. Always a learner!

I appreciate Ruth's ability to speak into my life by enabling me through my strong points rather than focusing in on areas where I may be weak. This has given me more confidence in desiring to grow more in my leadership skills. I have always loved her being a safe place in which to mature in leadership. There is always that little bit more to learn from Ruth."

Sandra Tjart
Former Director of World Partners Canada
Administrative Leader of Futures Team, Lincoln Heights EMC Church
Evangelical Missionary Church of Canada
Kitchener, Ontario

"Ruth Esau is a brilliant leadership facilitator and is a master of the teachable moment. Her book and leadership structure are both simple and creative. People who aspire to be leaders can gain a clear understanding, through her insights and questions, of the world, their organization, their staff and most of all, themselves. Building on the Self Leadership Framework developed over many years both in the field and facilitating groups, Ruth helps us to ask the right questions and to build a personal accountability growth path. She will turn the "Woe is me" into the "Whoa! It's me!" This book should be in every leader's toolbox."

John Rook, D. Phil (Oxford)
Managing Director (Calgary) & Director of Strategic Initiatives
The Mustard Seed Society
Calgary, Alberta

"Ruth is an expert at intentionally helping others to further grow and develop their own leadership skills for the transformation within the leader's contexts. Ruth has mastered the art of asking curious questions in order that you might deeply reflect and discover solutions to things that perplex and trip up leaders. She lets the wisdom in the room speak, while having the ability to guide us towards positive outcomes.

Ruth's influence has not only positively affected me in my varied leadership roles, but has had a trickledown effect on my marriage and family. I am a more competent, confident and optimistic leader because of the deeper learnings Ruth guided me to."

Alisa Jones
RN
Global Missions Director

"Ruth is a leader, founded in integrity, who gives of her knowledge and experience to support executive leaders understand how to leverage their skills, build their confidence, and create strong peer relationships as a means to more effectively manage their complex organizations."

Janet Mathieson
President and CEO
Wise Resources Inc
Human Resource Specialist

"Ruth Esau is a gifted leader. She communicates with confidence and asks questions that propel people in the direction of successful lives and ministries. She lives out a servant-hearted leadership style that affirms the people she coaches and teaches, while pointing them to choices based on God's truth that will enhance every aspect of their personal and spiritual growth. Her example inspires me to be a better leader."

Carol Kent
Executive Director of the Speak Up Conference
Author of *Speak Up with Confidence* (NavPress)

What-if Leadership Journal

The intentional pursuit of being, knowing and doing

Ruth Esau

EA Books Publishing
Oviedo, Florida

ISBN: 978-1-945976-57-5

Publisher's Cataloging-in-Publication data
Name: Esau, Ruth
Title: Title: Subtitle: What-if Leadership Journal/The intentional pursuit of being, knowing and doing. By Ruth Esau
Identifiers: LCCN: 2019916103
ISBN: 978-1-945976-57-5
Subjects: 1. BUS 074030 Business and Economics/Nonprofit Organizations and Charities/Management and Leadership
2. EDU 046000 Education/Professional Development
3. BUS 071000 Business and Economics/Leadership

Published by EA Books Publishing, a division of
Living Parables of Central Florida, Inc. a 501c3

EABooksPublishing.com

Dedication

What-if *Leadership Journal*
The intentional pursuit of being, knowing and doing

This book is dedicated to my dear friend and mentor, who chose to bless me with her mother's heart. Thank you Clara for believing in me, sharing your heart, your home, your admonishments and your wisdom with me. My life has been so much richer because of you. I so often hear Clara's voice, "Now Ruthie, you know…" Those words were always a precursor to wisdom that I needed to pay attention to and they were always delivered with straight forward truth and heartwarming love. I love you, Clara!

Table of Contents

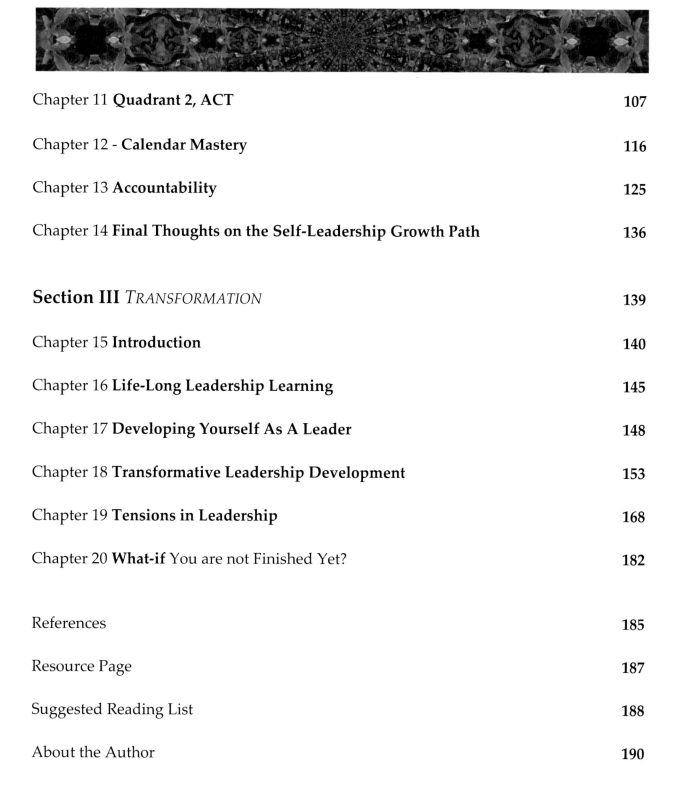

Preface

As a shy and quiet grade twelve student, little would I have imagined where I would be today. Back in the day we were admonished regularly, you must choose your education track carefully if you want to be successful. Those words are true and yet they have more than one perspective. I planned and prepared to be a nurse. Then came the rounds of applying for and being interviewed by three major training hospitals only to walk away broken-hearted, that because of a heart condition I did not pass the medical to become a nurse. I remember my family doctor shaking his head and saying, "If only you could do what you love with the heart and the passion you have, as well as taking nurses' training." All my preparation did not go in the direction I had prepared for and yet the process laid a foundation for developing resilience mentally and emotionally. As my plans shifted so did the opportunities that came my way. I cannot emphasize enough, that what you are passionate about does not come with a simple checklist for accomplishment. We gain knowledge in our studies, in living the life we have been given, whatever the circumstances are. And when we combine that, we discover we have unearthed a deep well of wisdom.

Life is a gift to be honoured and lived to the full. ***What-if*** *Leadership Journal* comes from such a life. It is a life that held limitations, challenges, disappointments, a magnitude of losses AND ALSO abundance, grace, opportunity, deep joy, success, failure, love and relational wealth. This is not one woman's leadership journey, this is the journey of a multitude of people who influenced her life in one way or another. I am so grateful for this journey together.

I encourage you to read and carve out the space to work through the curious questions provided. Some you will easily find answers to and some you will struggle with while wanting to chuck the book and say, "Forget it!" Some parts will meet you right where you are currently at and some you will wonder, "Why is this in this book?" My longing is that as you see yourself in different scenarios and grapple with many of the questions, you will find yourself deepened as a person. You will find yourself stronger, bolder, more reflective and resilient as a leader.

This book is written from the heart and mind of:

- *A visionary*-where many times my dreams are way bigger than the world I live in.

- *A visual learner and prototyper*-out of my visual learning style came a bent to turn my learnings into visuals for clarity and greater understanding.

- *A people person*-depth of relationship is of most importance to me.

- *An otter*-even the most tedious can be fun! Laughter heals the heart.

- *A strategist*-focus and reflection do lead to bold action with a few principles that create a firm foundation for decisions.

- *A realistic optimist*-at one time a Pollyanna, who refused to see any form of negativity and yet through the unsought school of pain, deep loss, focus and reflection, I found a way to build on the less than and become more.

I have been blessed to learn with and from so many. I have incorporated and adapted so many of those rich leanings into my context, life and leadership over the years. I have sought to acknowledge those whom I quoted directly and those whom I have adapted into my context. I apologize if there have been any oversights in acknowledging where everything I learned came from.

The stories I share are rich with challenges, experiences of failures, opportunities for growth by choosing to accept responsibility when pride often wanted to win, choosing to process and reflect rather than blame and become a victim. All of this was grace received and grace given. The journey of becoming has been offered to all of us.

Be inspired as you read, focus, reflect and move towards bold action.

Acknowledgments

A grateful heart is often marked by words of acknowledgment, even when the speaker or writer knows that the words are so inadequate to express the depth of investment that has been made. I am ever so aware of the clients, colleagues, staff, volunteers, bosses and friends I have had the privilege of serving with, of investing in, of entrusting leadership to. You are the ones that are the living proof of what happens as we bring the best of ourselves (and at times the less than the best of ourselves) together for a cause greater than ourselves. You are the heroes, the steadfast and resilient ones.

Thank you to those who were a part of incredible organizations and also were within my sphere of influence: Mayland Heights Church, Crossroads Community Church, Freckles Quilt Shop, Centre Street Church, First Alliance Church, Inspired to Lead Participants, Executive Directions - Summit cohort Executive Leaders in cohorts 4, 6, 7, 8, 9 and Ascent Second Level Executive Leaders in Cohorts 1, 2, 3. I loved and learned in my journey with each of you. Thank you for your gracious and generous wisdom and leadership courage.

Called to Lead and Leadership Savvy leaders, how do I thank the incredible people who came, listened, challenged, embraced and left more confident and competent than they had been before. I loved your heart to hear what was bubbling around in my mind at any point and time and making it richer and fuller than I would ever have dreamed. Thanks for being the dreamers and shapers with me.

Randy Reese, although you have gone to be with the Lord, many were the times you listened, you asked curious questions, you challenged and affirmed me. I am a part of the legacy you left behind.

Thank you to Carol Kent. You came into my life in the early 1980s and that began a much more adventurous and courageous journey of saying yes, and moving out of my comfort zone.

Thank you to Cheri Cowell and EA Books Publishing who offered me an opportunity to learn, to hone and finally, to write a book.

Thank you to the team of dedicated, knowledgeable and awesome EA Books Publishing Staff who mentored and taught me and answered every simplistic question I asked - Peter Lundgren, Michelle Booth, Marjorie Vawter, Laurie and John Copeland, Kristen Veldhuis, Jessie Collins and Krystine Kercher.

Joanne Wiens, my dear friend and editor extraordinaire. Thank you is so small for your generous and wise spirit that made this all come together.

In October, 2019, I lost my colleague, mentor and friend, Corey Olynik. I am so grateful for all you saw in me and called out in me. Your legacy carries on, in and through all those you invested in.

My parents, Russ and Wilma, who invested beyond measure to provide space for love, health, healing, learning and growth. You laid the foundations I have been privileged to build upon. I miss you and your love and wisdom daily.

My family, who had many of these principles practiced on them over the years! And these are the ones, the dear ones, whose faces stand before me in each decision I make. I love each of you beyond measure.

Brian, who knew when we said yes to each other 47 years ago that we would survive and thrive on our journey together? You truly have always been the wind beneath my heart and feet. Thank you for your faithful, loving ways that have pushed me, encouraged me and been there in all our comings and goings. I love you!

May each of your lives be as enriched by our times together as mine has been by each of you.

I am most grateful!

How to Use This Book

Welcome to **What-if** *Leadership Journal*. Just by picking it up, you agree to go on an adventure that has the potential to deepen your character and increase your leadership skills. The choice is yours with each page you engage in and each page you turn. Will you leave the challenges behind or will you rise to meet them right where it may be most uncomfortable?

What-if *Leadership Journal* is set up to encourage you to do some deep thinking as well as the processing of the information as you engage in the material and seek to place it into your leadership context personally and professionally. This material is not about sitting in a comfy chair and reading it from cover to cover. Please read, pause and ponder, put it down and think long and hard about the questions. Think about yourself, who you want to be as a leader and how you want to create a life-giving and sustainable leadership development culture. Then get out and talk about it with others and broaden your perspective and influence with others for good.

Section 1 starts with you as a leader. What do you think, believe, expect and do? What is the foundation for your decisions and actions?

Section 2 challenges you to do the hard work of pulling all your knowledge, experience, doubts and dreams together in order to move to that future that you know can be yours.

Section 3 makes space for the freedom to let go and to pour into others. Your leadership is about the now and yet it is also about sustainability for the future by what you choose to invest in and entrust to others.

Spend time with what resonates with you most. Take the time to reflect, engage and move out of your comfort zone and be amazed at where you will go. Invite and bring others along with you, building on their wisdom and experience to deepen and broaden what is and what will be.

Each section will continue to challenge your self-awareness, your other awareness. It will take time to reflect and make sense of the principles in your context and you may find it just may not look like everyone else's leadership persona. Take the time to find and develop your best self, for the sake of a world that cries for integrity, authenticity, meaning and fulfillment amid chaos and fast paced expectations.

Section 1—*INSPIRATION*

Contents

Introduction

What-if Leadership

What-if? Just **What-if** a slight movement or turn would create a shift in our thinking that freed us to see from a new perspective and make space for fresh momentum?

At age three, I was stricken with sudden onset of rheumatic fever, which meant I was in the hospital for a lengthy stay and then in bed for almost a year. How do you entertain a curious, spunky (on the inside) three-year-old? Toys and gifts were intended to entertain in a small confined space, namely a brown metal-barred crib.

One gift I received was a kaleidoscope. I loved it, especially on days when my crib was moved outside or close to the kitchen window. I loved the beauty I would see through the eyepiece. If I moved the kaleidoscope up to the sky, the colours were vibrant and bright; if I pointed it down to the blankets, the colours were more subdued and gentler. If I got tired of the pattern, I would see what the tiniest twist would reveal and shift the design. I would see something I had not seen before.

As an adult immersed in leadership, kaleidoscopes came into my life again as I sought to make some leadership principles understandable to those in my sphere of influence. If I changed the direction the kaleidoscope faced or made a small twist, it could produce something so different, something new. Could that be a metaphor I could use to bring understanding to those times we get stuck in leadership situations that seem impossible? As I analyzed the makeup of a kaleidoscope, I made some other wonderful discoveries. The ever-changing beauty of a kaleidoscope comes from the many broken pieces of glass as well as the light and mirrors needed to shift to new or different patterns.

Leadership has many universal principles that apply no matter what our role, situation, relationships, or context. And when we get stuck, they just need a little change of direction and/or focus to reveal what possibilities lie ahead.

The *kaleidoscope* has become a metaphor for so much in my leadership.

I don't know what I don't know! **What-if** I allowed for a shift in my perspective? Wow! Look what I see now!

Failure is not the end! **What-if** I used my mistakes or failures as a leader to launch me to new or different levels of influence?

Reflections keep us true to the higher purpose. **What-if** I made time for intentional reflection, weighing what is with what could be? Where might it take me?

Gradually then suddenly! **What-if** I slowly took time to look at what creates fear in me? A slight twist and wow! I didn't see that coming! Beautiful!

In conversation with a dear friend and colleague one day, Jayne told me the story of working as a member of an Executive Council through a dramatic situation that threatened the institution's leadership and as a result the entire organization. Unhappy with the lack of concrete action by the Executive Council and especially the Chair, Jayne prepared a document offering advice and concrete steps that she felt would move the situation forward. Before pressing Send she shared the document with a seasoned leader. He listened to the story, read the document, and then asked one question: "**What-if** this letter was written in such a way that it made the Chair a better leader?"

As Jayne shared this with me I could feel all the inner alerts firing up within me, most of them were rather dramatic and full of emotional waste. I felt the desire to justify the need for someone to be corrected, the need to be right, the need to patronize the one who didn't get it, just to name a few. As I reflected on how I felt and how that made everything seem so overblown, I realized that it was exactly that emotional response and then acting on that level of strong emotion that causes us to get stuck, to be unable to move forward.

I began to look at what holds us back as leaders. What gets us stuck in dark places that diminish our leadership influence? I began to look at all kinds of scenarios I coach clients through and began to craft **What-if** questions that would be able to move them forward.

Questions like:

What-if you had a conversation that focused on the other person becoming a better leader?

What-if you led a company where your clients, staff and volunteers raved about their experience?

What-if you approached difficult situations with the expected outcome to be growth?

What-if roles, expectations and accountability were created in a way that employees could think for themselves and problem solve without running to you all the time?

What-if conversations you overheard on a regular basis were such that the give and take of healthy relationships trumped drama, ego and emotional waste?

What-if there was a way to lead that used diversity as a stepping-stone to unity?

What-if you knew how to shift the energy that mental battles take from you?

What-if you led in a leadership world where emotion was harnessed to collaborate with the facts and realistic optimism was generous and lavish?

What-if you were able to sift through which of your thoughts and feelings were true and discard the rest?

What-if you were equipped to choose the better over what is easy?

What-if you were developing rhythms of life that allowed you to lead in all areas of your life with focus and energy?

What-if you had the kinds of relationships that energized and made you a better person and leader?

What-if as a leader you could get out of your own way and continually move to the big picture and why that matters?

What-if you knew what it meant to lead from a base of authenticity?

Then I began to look at **What-if** Values.

What-if you became a MORE INTENTIONAL LEADER?

What-if you became a MORE REFLECTIVE LEADER?

What-if you became a MORE CURIOUS LEADER?

What-if you became a BOLDER LEADER?

What-if you became a MORE CONFIDENT LEADER?

What-if you became a MORE COMPETENT LEADER?

What-if you became a MORE TRUSTWORTHY LEADER?

What-if you became a MORE INTEGRATED LEADER?

What-if you became a MORE PURPOSEFUL LEADER?

What-if you became a MORE VALUES DRIVEN LEADER?

What-if you became a MORE RELATIONAL LEADER?

What-if you became a MORE FOCUSED LEADER?

What-if you became a MORE INSPIRED LEADER?

I considered what it would take to be one of those values driven leaders, to experience the powerful and positive energy that would be created and how that would lead in a very different and positive direction. I thought about the decrease in stress from dwelling in negative energy. I also pondered stopping that negative energy that eats away at your clarity of thought, your mindfulness, your quality of sleep and your well-being.

The contrast is profound. A perspective shift creates a space for getting rid of the old ways of negative thinking, old patterns of defeat, emotional waste and time-wasting drama. With a slight turn in your thinking you are able to find new wells of energy to draw from to discover a greater quality of life and leadership. And so, I found myself eager and ready to pursue the concept of **What-if Leadership?**

I began to see how well it connected with my leadership purpose statement:

Intentionally inspiring leaders to focus, to reflect, and to take bold action.

Chapter 1
The Story of Inspired to Lead

In our leadership journey, it is a series of seemingly small steps that eventually take us to that place where our talents and opportunities intersect, to that place where we find our true calling. My story is about inspiration. Let's step back a little into my leadership formation and history.

In spite of growing up with a life-limiting heart condition and being an introvert, most of my life I have been entrusted with leadership in one form or another. As a teenager and a young adult, I literally trembled at getting up in front of people. As a fourteen-year-old when I was asked to answer the phone, I would say to my mom, "Well, what will I say?" When Mom encouraged me to consider being a teacher, I would look at her, scrunch my nose and raise my eyebrows and say, "I could never stand in front of people and have their hairy eyeballs staring back at me!" When you realize that this was back in the 60s and 70s, the term leadership was not applied to those things that I did! I did not see myself as a leader.

And yet in hindsight I realize that as a young person I held many emerging leadership roles in club, camp and church settings. Later I was entrusted with all kinds of volunteer leadership roles in the church—some of these terms you may never have heard of - like small group leader and trainer, disciple-maker and trainer, kids' club leader, mentor, volunteer trainer and manager. I had the privilege of co-managing a great little quilt shop. There were also paid roles in the church such as life formation pastor, women's ministry pastor, leadership development pastor, serve pastor. For another twelve years I facilitated and coached executive level leaders in the nonprofit sector. My adult life had been filled with leadership roles and responsibilities. Throughout this time formal and informal learning and development took place.

Prior to heading into the work world, we (our family of three teenagers, Brian, and myself) were on a wonderful family holiday on Vancouver Island. I had been so privileged to be a full-time mom. As the kids hit the teen years, I had wondered about what I would do with the increase of discretionary time that I faced as they grew older. At one of our meals together, the kids began to tease me about getting out and seeing if anyone would hire me! We are a family of laughter and humour not allowing ourselves to be taken too seriously! So I said I would rise to that challenge when we got home!

The previous fall I had taken some quilting classes and after this summer vacation I popped down to a wonderful little quilt store called Freckles to buy some material to start a quilt for one of my daughters. As the owner, Jenny, measured out my fabric and we had casual give and take of snapshots of our lives, Jenny casually said to me, "Have you ever thought of going back to work?"

WOW! *BOOM!* **BANG!**

I almost burst out laughing! I told her about our family conversation and said I had been thinking of it. On the spot Jenny offered me a job. Oh my! As I walked out of Freckles my mind was whirring. How would I present this at supper? I made a lovely supper with a few extra touches! Imagine a huge grin that could not be wiped off my face as I prepared! We sat down and began our meal. It was then I so casually dropped the information on the table that I had been hired that day without writing a resumé, or even going job hunting! Imagine that moment of delight I had and the look of surprise and then giggling congratulations from my kids and hubby! Oh so fun!

Both Jenny and I knew that this was a season that we would be in together, and we believed that both of us would know when we were to end this season. That began a nine-year journey at Freckles. It started with learning the art of quilting to quickly becoming a co-manager, with twenty-two employees. I was hungry to learn more. I took courses from the Business Development Bank, Stephen Covey, Business Management Courses, Human Resource Courses, and Speak Up With Confidence. These courses came just in time for learning helpful tools for the situations I was entrusted to handle at work.

One day I contacted Jenny to go for lunch. I knew that it was time for me to close the chapter on Freckles in a hired role. Jenny resounded with, "I was just going to call you!" And so we booked a lunch together. As we sat face-to-face, we both realized we had something to say to each other that was significant. I deferred to Jenny, and as I did Jenny shared that the time had come for her and her husband David to sell Freckles. Huh! I could hardly sit there as I too shared that I knew it was time for me to leave Freckles. We actually had known this when we began to work together. We had said something like we both knew we would know when the time would come to part from our working days together.

As I left Freckles I wondered what lay ahead. I spent a year and a half reflecting and measuring what life was and where it could be. And then came a wonderful opportunity that opened a new chapter for me at Centre Street Church in Calgary, Alberta. At this time Centre Street Church was one of the largest churches in Canada. I was invited in to explore what it would be like to become the Director of Women's Ministries. It started as a volunteer role, working with women who led various programs for other women. I spent ten years at Centre Street Church, quickly moving into a Senior Pastor Role. Again, this provided an opportunity for embracing the "just in time" learning and recognizing so much of what was intuitive in my leadership. I flourished in being able to now use this knowledge to raise up others to their full leadership potential. It allowed me to explain to someone else what came so intuitively to me. I watched programs morph from being focused on maintaining programs, to developing people and giving them the space to become all they were created to be.

I referred earlier that as a young child I suffered a severe case of rheumatic fever, which left my mitral valve damaged and scar tissue on my heart. I was in the hospital for a long period of time and then confined to bed for a year. My parents later told me how doctors said I probably would not live to go to school. My parents' faith and courage embraced this news and the lifestyle it created for them while choosing to live life to the full. I know I do not fully appreciate the sacrifices they made to give me life, and yet I am most grateful. I did not ever think of my life in terms of limitations because of their great outlook.

I did live within those limitations, which as an adult created disappointment that I learned to overcome. I loved sports, but the strain on my heart was too great. I only ever wanted to be a nurse, and yet after applying to three nursing schools, I was rejected each time because my heart was inadequate to handle the strain. Brian and I wanted to have four children, but we were told after our third child was born that if we decided to have a fourth child the chances were extremely high my husband would be left with three, maybe four, children to raise and no mother. And yet those disappointments became a foundation I learned to build my life upon: to find joy and meaning in what I did have rather than what I did not have. Even though I was raised in a family with a strong faith who believed that God could do the impossible, I never thought to ask God to heal my heart.

Fast forward to 1999. In 2000 I would turn fifty. As I went for my yearly physical in June 1999, my doctor expressed the need to do a battery of tests to affirm what shape my heart was in so we could address what the years ahead might hold. These tests were booked for the end of September 1999. During the first week of September that year I was on a staff retreat out in the country. As we drove home, I developed an excruciating pain in my stomach. I had NO sleep that night. The next day I saw my doctor, only to have to wait another forty-eight hours for test results. The next night the pain was unbearable, so my doctor sent me to an emergency clinic to get checked out. After being examined, the doctor left the room saying he would be right back. As I lay on the examining table, I had a burst of pain and then things seemed to be so much better. I gingerly got up and got dressed. I was so embarrassed to think I had just had an abundance of indigestion and gas. The doctor came in and asked, "What are you doing?" I replied, "I am so embarrassed. I think I just had really bad indigestion and gas. There was a burst of pain and my stomach is tender, but the pain is gone!" The doctor said, "I was booking a hospital bed and surgery for you and now I know you need it for sure." What? The doctor said, "I am pretty sure you have an abscessed, perforated appendix, and I would say now it has burst. With your heart condition, you need to have antibiotics and surgery right away. We can call an ambulance, or your husband can drive you to the hospital. You are not to stop at home. The hospital is waiting for you."

Stunned, Brian drove me to Foothills Hospital. I lay on the stretcher, surrounded with IV bags of saline and antibiotics. The next morning, they wheeled me into the operating room. There were three doctors around my bed. The surgeon at the end of the bed asked where my husband was, as he did not want to do the surgery without Brian nearby.

As I raised my head from the pillow, I said he had gone home to get rest as he had been up all night. The surgeon to my right took my face in his hands and said, "You realize that your chances of survival are extremely slim!" In my head, there was FEAR on a mega scale. It was then I sensed the presence of Jesus right beside me and He said, "I have a mantle of peace for you. Do you want it?" The fear was immediately right sized, and I let my head flop back on the pillow as I said to the doctors, "My life is in your hands." The doctor at the foot of the bed pointed upwards and said, "And in His?" I said yes. They wheeled me into surgery.

In the days after the surgery, I had a myriad of heart residents come to see me and their recommendation was that I would need to have open heart surgery sooner rather than later. My inner voice was screaming: "Really! I haven't got over this surgery! I don't want to think about another one!" I was released after a week. As I came home, I noticed something was different— I had an abundance of energy. Brian commented to me that he had never known me with such energy, and this was in spite of being in recuperating mode. Off the cuff I said, "Maybe I have always had an infected appendix!" Three weeks later I went for the heart tests that had been booked for me back in June, long before I knew I had any appendix issues. I asked the technician, "Do you see any problems with my heart?" She replied, "I should not say anything, but I am wondering why you are having these tests. You have the heart of a sixteen-year-old!" Really? Hmmm!

As I went for my follow up appointment to the surgeon, I discovered he was an atheist. Hmmm, so many dots to connect. An atheist who acknowledged there was someone higher than himself and who had been in charge of my surgery! I went to my family doctor for a follow up to the heart tests. She asked me to sit down and said, "I don't know how to tell you this, but your heart is completely whole. There is no scar tissue left and your mitral valve is fully functioning." I asked if she could explain it and she said no! She continued to say, "I don't believe in God, but there are times we cannot explain what has happened." She laughed and said, "Maybe you never had a heart condition!" Then she lifted my file up and said, "But we have all the evidence here!"

Wow! As I continued to recover, I pondered this gift of life and what it would mean now to live with purpose and values in the light of the gift I had been granted. I now had life like I had never experienced before. I no longer had heaviness in my chest or shortness of breath when I exerted myself. I was no longer exhausted all the time. Life changed! I came to value the second chance I had been given in a new way. I became value driven. I began to teach and help my people and my teams define and embrace values. We learned what it meant to focus on values and to deal with personal hurts in a value driven way. We thrived in the work that we did together.

About three months later, Brian and I were driving home late at night from a staff Christmas party. It had been a stormy night and we had an hour and a half drive home. We came over the hill to see a glare of black ice and cars in the ditch. Somehow, Brian gripped the wheel. We went off the road and into the ditch and miraculously back up on to the road. A few moments later Brian said, "You are pretty quiet. Are you okay?" I said, "I just saw my life flash before my eyes, and I was talking to God. 'Really, God, you just healed my heart and now you are going to take me like this?' His gentle response was, 'I healed your heart and you must realize you are not going to live forever!'"

Ah, perspective, a twist of the kaleidoscope to face my expectations and the current reality!

While I was still at Centre Street Church in the summer of 2005, I was given a wonderful opportunity for my husband, Brian, and I to use a condo on beautiful Lake Okanagan. It was to be time for renewal and refreshing physically, mentally, emotionally, and spiritually. Just days before we were to leave, Brian had a work complication that meant he could not go with me.

I wasn't sure I wanted to go on my own as I had never spent an entire week all by myself in a city where I did not know anyone. Yikes! What would that be like? There would be no one to talk to or to see the sights with! That sounded rather bleak and scary! The fact of the matter is that I can get lost in a paper bag! These were the days before GPS. I used a good old paper map that was large and unwieldy as my guide. At the last minute our eldest daughter, Melodie, offered to drive out with me for the weekend and then fly home on Sunday evening. We had a wonderful weekend of sightseeing and great food and relaxation.

On Sunday evening as I arrived at the condo after dropping Mel off at the airport, I had an inner restlessness that would not go away. I walked down to the lake and back. I had a glass of lemonade and came inside to sit on the couch. There on the coffee table was a book I had picked up three months earlier and yet had not even opened. I was drawn to it as it had a white cover and every letter of the title was a different colour in a fun script. I had been hooked and bought it. As I sat on the couch, sipping lemonade, I picked up the book and began to flip through it.

It was called *Inspire!* by Lance Secretan. As I flipped through the book, I came to read the definition of *inspire* that Secretan quotes from Webster's dictionary.

> The word is derived from the Latin root word spirare meaning "spirit," to breathe, to give life—the breath of God.

> Webster's says that to inspire is like "breathing in, as in air to the lungs; to infuse with an encouraging or exalting influence; to animate; stimulation by divinity, a genius, an idea or a passion; a divine influence upon human beings."

I was captured by the thought that I would actually look up to something bigger than myself and be enabled to receive fresh inspiration for whatever I was to be and to do. It wasn't just a nice thought. It was an actual way of receiving something that was more than myself and then having something of worth to offer others to be inspired. I saw myself on my knees with my face lifted heavenward, arms extended and feeling the fresh breath of God's Holy Spirit breathing new life into me. Then in turn I was able to turn to meet others where they were and breathe fresh life and encouragement into them. That would be of far greater worth than what I could give them on my own. You might say that inspiration is a soul journey. It comes from my very inner being that is in touch with the God who created me. From that comment alone you will understand that I come from a biblical worldview that believes in creation and God. You may not have this same worldview. This does not mean that this should divide us even if our beliefs are different. It does mean we have the opportunity to travel a part of our journey together in order to make each other better leaders.

What-if the difference in our beliefs actually was a stepping-stone to each of us becoming better leaders, to learning from others what we do not know or have not yet learned?

After ten years, I made the decision to leave Centre Street Church. I had come to the place where I knew my heart's passion was to create spaces of safety, academics, praxis, relationship and accountability so others could rise to their full potential as leaders. In my leaving, I did not know what that would look like, or where I was going.

In 2007, while launching out to create and develop my new business/ministry *Inspired to Lead*, I continued to learn. I took courses from Coach Training Alliance, Talent Smart and Renovoir. I avidly read so many incredible books to understand why something mattered and if it did matter, what could that mean if I grasped it, if I lived it and if I passed it on to others. As my learning increased in the midst of leadership responsibilities, I discovered that even though there were places where I got stuck, there also were ample resources for getting unstuck.

What-if the challenges that appear to you as interruptions actually were preparing you to face where you are stuck and to discover ways of getting unstuck and deepening your leadership effectiveness and confidence?

I invite you to continue to journey on with me from here and to take a deeper look at your own leadership history and development.

Notes—record your most significant thoughts to reflect on and to begin bold action.

Chapter 2

What Holds Us Back?

For each of us who have been entrusted with a leadership role, our hearts are to live with purpose. We want to make a difference, to live beyond our own personal limitations, to serve a greater good. In actuality we are called to make a difference with our lives. For me, that bigger purpose is a belief in God, God with a capital G. The God who created the world and who loved the world enough that He sent His one and only Son Jesus to give us life and to give it more abundantly.

What-if rather than stop reading now because you believe something different than I do, you kept reading and brought your strengths and wisdom to this conversation?

What-if by our differences we become like iron sharpening iron and we are enabled to make a bigger difference for good in our world?

This diagram stands for a picture of our relationship with someone or something bigger than ourselves while interconnecting with others. In the leadership roles and responsibilities you hold, take a moment to form these thoughts into your worldview or your perspective.

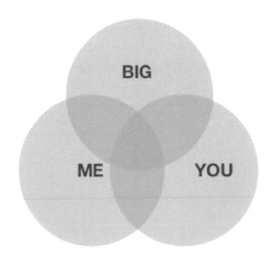

Kaleidoscope Reflections

1. As a leader how would you describe what you consider to be bigger than yourself? How would you describe that person, that calling, or that purpose?

2. When you think of this bigger image you hold and who you are, describe what is in this that resonates with who you are?

3. As you consider this bigger image or purpose, who you are and what you would need from others, describe what you sense is needed to accomplish this purpose.

Expectations

In anything we consider, whether it be a situation or a particular relationship, we come with expectations that are based on our experience, education and numerous other influences. These expectations can be spoken or unspoken; they represent our *PERSPECTIVES*. They are the way we experience life and leadership and are the lens through which we see. This would be like what we see when we first look into a kaleidoscope.

We may have the same purpose as someone else and yet our perspective on it can have many differences. We take our perspectives as truth, that this is the way and at times we may think the only way! As we work with others, we discover there may be many perspectives on the same concept. Some of those perspectives will make the concept so much better, and other perspectives will cause a dissonance in us as this was not in sync with our perspective. This is when we bump up against current reality.

Current Reality

Current reality is the actual way things are and the challenges and opportunities that go with that reality. We often find there is a gap between what we expect expressed in our perspective and then what truly is in our current reality.

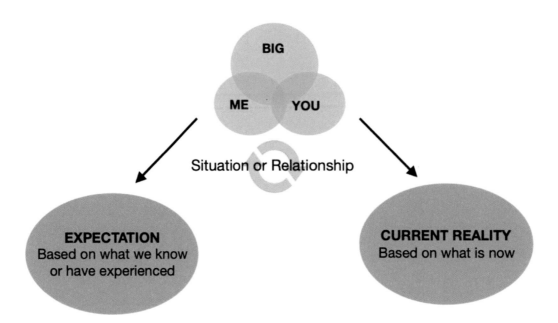

Recently I watched the miniseries on Netflix called *The Crown*, the story of Queen Elizabeth and the Commonwealth. I had watched it before and enjoyed engaging in a history that is a part of my story. This time as I watched, I focused on Queen Elizabeth herself, who is the longest reigning female leader in the world. Now yes, that was her place to fill by process and precedent and yet she also could have been deposed as other royalty had been before her. Watching the Queen through leadership eyes was fascinating to me. I saw a pattern in her leadership that has served her well.

I would say it could be described in the following words:

Composed, prepared, hospitable, respectful, a believer in the best of others, curious, listener, appreciative, gracious in inviting to reality, focused on moving forward in spite of the challenges, values driven.

And then there are words that would describe how she became that kind of leader:

Study, reflection, willing to learn, success and failure in spades, open to feedback, experienced criticism and hurt, focused on the important, accepting of her own humanity and the humanity of others.

Am I thinking I see a perfect leader? No, I see a leader who has stepped out of her comfort zone, succeeded, failed, tried again, risen above failure by facing it and dealing with it. She is a leader who deeply cares and focuses on a purpose far greater than herself. She is no different than any one of us in many ways and yet she is on public display where public opinion speaks with few filters. In many scenes of her life, others' expectations and the current reality she saw were in stark contrast. They had the potential for misunderstanding, pain and hurt. When this clash happened between expectations and current reality, a trigger event occurred that she became very adept at navigating.

When our expectations bump up against current reality, we call that a *trigger event*. Trigger events generally surface because they hit at one of our values and create an inner ouch. We experience dissonance which often hits like a lightning bolt that slams us mid-chest where our heart is.

What-if I learned to live in expectancy rather than with expectations?

This became a powerful concept for me. Expectations come from my perspective on any given situation or person that I find myself involved with. I read the situation from what I have experienced in the past, what I know and what I perceive. This will often trigger emotions because a different value is revealed as taking precedent in someone else's experience.

Once my emotions are triggered, I can so readily begin to make up stories in my head that usually are not true. They may have a ring of truth, but they are not reliable.

What does it look like to be triggered by our emotions? As a young mom, my mom was diagnosed with a brain tumour, which turned out to be an inoperable cancer. The tumour was in the part of her brain that related to the ability to feel pain. The miracle of that was she did not experience any pain in the short six weeks before she passed away.

In the midst of this experience of loss, grief and mourning, I realized my brain began to play tricks on me by trying to convince me that when I got a headache, I concluded I probably had a brain tumour! This would trigger my emotion of fear, which gave credence to that story. What happened to me was called beguilement. In hindsight I realized that the facts of the situation were that my mom had no pain or headaches with her brain tumour. And yet because of the strength of my emotion of fear, if I had a headache, I felt it must be a brain tumour. I went with my emotional response of fear rather than with the facts.

As a leader I experienced this many times. I also experienced my assumptions and expectations challenged. On one occasion when I was hired in a particular leadership role, I entered in having read the role description and the organizational expectations. I had a few interviews where Q&A were open and transparent. And then I became a part of an incredible organization. Over time as I listened and interacted, I became more familiar with what I would call the 'unspoken family rules.' In the long game for me these unspoken family rules did not mesh with who I was or how I worked best. I had to STOP-REFLECT- RECALCULATE. I had to address the organization's unspoken expectations, my boss's way of being and his expectations, who I was and how I contributed best. The end result was my leaving this role and choosing to bless them for what they do. I was now free to find the place I could offer my best that would align with the role I was to move into next.

As a leader you may have other stories. They are stories of what you were told to expect and then finding out what the current reality was. Perhaps you have had to navigate situations where lack of clarity created spaces for trigger events to happen and hurt to ensue. These are the opportunities for deep and meaningful leadership learning.

Trigger Events

What-if there was a way to recognize when your emotions are making a situation bigger than it needs to be?

Our way to experience the world is through our senses. We experience life through our sight, taste, smell, hearing and touch. This comes into our brains through our brain stem as raw data, which has not yet been refined. Our brain is a marvelous organ. Once we sense something, we can have a very real, highly emotional response, which is like a trigger being pulled. The response can make us strong, make us bold, and also has the potential to make us volatile.

The concept of Ready . . . Aim . . . Fire can very easily become Fire . . . Fire . . . Fire! Or if we are startled by a concept we may withdraw and only Aim . . . Aim . . . Aim!

When our processing of these events and our emotions is faulty, then these trigger events have the potential for causing hurt or pain, depending on how we choose to experience them and process them. So often the way we take these events becomes a personal offence and is the cause of a far greater hurt and pain than is necessary.

Our brain was created to process the raw data through the limbic portion, which is the emotion centre of the brain. The work of the brain does not stop there as the information in the limbic portion of the brain must travel to the frontal cortex, which includes the executive suite made up of the factual functions of the brain. When this conversation continues to go back and forth, it combines our emotions and the facts into a healthy stream of thought and ultimately healthy behaviours. When this healthy conversation does not happen, we become stuck quite typically inside our own heads, which affects the way we see and the way we choose to behave and lead. We find ourselves caught between our expectations and current reality, which may appear very different and set off a trigger event which can be highly emotional to start with.

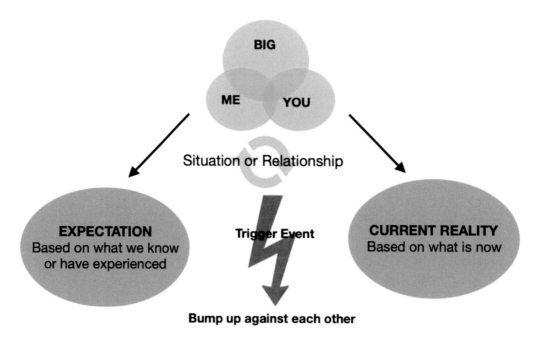

For me, what I see can be a simple trigger that left unattended will lead to a far bigger reaction than the situation warrants. I was doing contract work for a company which involved my passing on all the administrative workload that I had been responsible for. I could hardly wait as administration is not my strong suit. I do it because it is important to the outcomes I desire to see. One simple little task was to create tent cards with participants' names. I had shown a sample, acknowledged I knew the logo would change and left the names for the new tent cards. The morning of our first cohort, I entered the room, the tent cards were present. There was no logo and the font was too small to be useful for all to see. An internal hot button was pushed. My internal dialogue was about how could such a simple and clear task be done so wrong? From my perspective that hot button was a "pay attention" moment for me to STOP- REFLECT- RECALCULATE. I made the best of the tent cards for the day and I chose to refrain from apologizing for them and laying blame. After the cohort was finished, I went to the administrator and addressed the fact that I had left some information out that would have been helpful for her and showed her what I wanted in a name plate. It was a simple conversation rather than a conflict.

Learning to pay attention to what creates a trigger response inside me has provided healthier ways of dealing with potential situations of conflict. A principle I pay attention to is whether this is a one-off situation, or after a similar situation happens three times, it is now a pattern that is unacceptable. It is better to address the situation the first time with clarity and calmness while it is a conversation. This allows everyone to move forward rather than letting it go until a negative pattern is formed, where you become overly ticked and the conversation becomes heated. This is a very simple example. I have also experienced times when simple examples like this have led to much bigger confrontations than are required. Self-awareness leads to understanding others more clearly, as well as learning to lead through situations rather than reacting more strongly than is necessary.

 Kaleidoscope Reflections

1. Think of a recent time when you experienced a highly emotional response to a situation. Describe that scenario. Was it a one-time situation or had a pattern already formed?

2. Describe what creates a negative trigger for you.

3. When you look back to your upbringing, what were acceptable attitudes and behaviours around trigger events?

4. How has this influenced how you handle trigger events as a leader?

5. What is the downside of this response and what is one thing you could try to rewire in your brain for healthier interactions when your emotions are high?

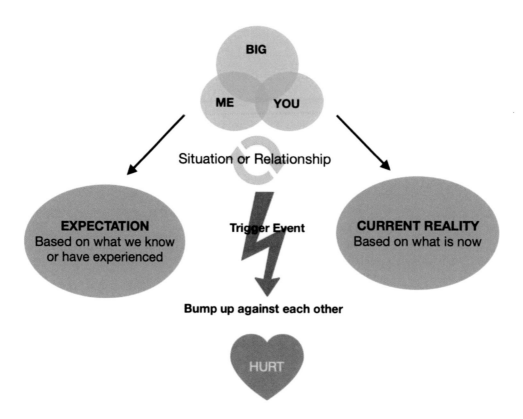

Hurt

"Personal breakthroughs begin with change in beliefs, because your beliefs determine your expectations, and your expectations determine your action."

John Maxwell

Expectations can create an environment for hurt to thrive. There are times when from our perspective, our expectations are pretty clear, and yet we may also slip some assumptions into those expectations. This creates a decrease in clarity around the situation. When our expectations are not met and at times our assumptions get mixed in with our expectations, we have the potential to take it personally and to experience hurt.

What-if knowing what to do with criticism served to make us better leaders?

As we step into any form of leadership, we now have eyes on us that bring different perspectives to our world than we may have had before. Those perspectives come with the particular filters that each person has experienced life through and to them their perspective is right.

There are times in our leadership journey we forget that although people have invited us into a role, or hired us for a role for certain characteristics, skills, qualities and abilities, we do not have all that particular role will need to be successful and achieve the best possible outcome. Leadership by nature calls for team, for a broad network of varying views, gifts, abilities, characteristics and strengths. This results in a much fuller and wider success than what any one person can bring on their own.

Growth requires change; change makes people uncomfortable. It takes a different focus than the status quo. It requires the desire to rise above mediocrity. Change triggers emotion that if raw has the potential to create drama and emotional waste around the required change. The end result is resistance, which often comes in the form of criticism for what was or what another person considers the right way. When delivered inappropriately and when taken personally, criticism has the power to paralyze us and get us stuck in negativity or even a victim mentality. We feel there is nothing we can do and this is all unfair. Leadership knows that preparing head and heart and asking for people's viewpoints whether they see eye to eye or not, will allow for a greater and fuller experience and end result.

As a leader, **What-if** you were offensive about criticism rather than defensive?

What-if as a leader you were proactive about criticism rather than reactive?

These are easy concepts to deal with on paper and they will also be the greatest challenges of our leadership over time.

One of my profound mentors taught me a healthy way to be proactive with criticism. Rather than waiting for criticism to come, which it surely will, be active in your relationships by asking two questions. As you see me in this season, or this situation, or in this relationship:

What do you want to celebrate about me?
What do you want to caution me about?

Being open to this kind of feedback enables you to come to the situation with an openness to receive feedback, even tough, feedback Your role is to learn to truly listen to the feedback you are given, keep it factual, choose not to make it personal, in order to be accountable and grow.

 Kaleidoscope Reflections

1. To keep from taking it personally, allow yourself to receive feedback through your senses (raw data), name how it makes you feel, and move to the facts that are being presented.

2. Reflect on how you can use what you are feeling to move you forward in the situation in light of the facts, rather than get stuck in the power of the emotion.

Know that in asking for feedback, taking time to reflect on what has been given to you is so important. Then for healthy accountability, go back to the person when you are ready to have the conversation around what you learned from their feedback and discuss what you plan on doing with it to move forward.

Criticism is at the very beginning of hurt. It moves to hurt when we allow that criticism to go unattended and we take what is said personally based on our raw emotions. Hurt in any form that is not handled well will only deepen with time and increase in intensity.

In one of my leadership roles, I was given the mandate to deal with a forty-year unsupervised situation in an organization that no one wanted to address. The new broom in the organization (myself) was given the mandate to bring this program and the leaders in it into line with the new and more clarified direction of the organization. I was given the advice, "Do not shoot a sacred cow; either help it find full health or help it die with dignity." As you may perceive, this was not a great win/win situation to be entrusted with as a newbie in the organization. Slowly and with much reflection, I began to address the situation. I immediately received resistance because I was an unknown and I was messing with something that was important and even precious to the leadership of this program. I cast vision, I sought to build relationship, I volunteered to help, I ensured they got their budget protected and received. You know I did all the things I knew to do. And so I expected that:

if I built relationship we would talk about difficulties and work them out;

if I gave clear information, it would be embraced and followed;

if I was given this mandate, I would also be supported in carrying it out.

You know the drill. You can name your own situation that will have different nuances to it and yet you will recognize it!

One day as I came in for work, I was met by my supervisor and told that I would need to appear before a grievance committee that would be assembling in the boardroom with ten additional women who had a complaint against me on this certain day and time. WHAT? What was going on? You guessed it! I wasn't clear on the details of the complaint, and yet I had a pretty good idea of who some of the people involved might be. I was puzzled. How could something get to this stage and no one had yet had a conversation with me? I expected that if people had grievances, there was a healthy process. This did not feel healthy to me! I pondered and reflected and prepared for what I wasn't really clear about and felt my role was to go and listen. I stopped in at my office and picked up some big fat folders of all that I had documented and was working with in this situation and went back to my supervisor's office. I asked, "I am curious, why has no one asked to hear my perspective in this situation? These are the files I have kept." I was told to leave them on the desk, and they would be looked at before we were to meet in the boardroom in an hour. I was to go back to my office and would be called when they were ready for me.

The meeting happened. Information, attitudes and feelings were put on the table. I listened. At one point one of the women stood up to say that if she had known this was a witch hunt, she would have not come. She was told to sit down. When asked if I had anything to say I responded with, "I don't know how this got as far as it did. Please know that if you ever have a question, comment, grievance, pick up the phone and say, 'Let's talk.'" The chairman of the grievance committee rose to speak and informed the room that I was exonerated and if there were any more complaints of this kind, those complaining would be removed from their volunteer positions. I was asked to remain seated while everyone left the room. After everyone left, I walked down the hall, walked in front of the door to my supervisor's office, stuck my head in and said, "This is not over you know." I glanced out the window to the parking lot and sure enough, there were the women continuing the conversation. I was invited into the room and as I stepped in, I heard a grievance committee member say, "See I told you she wasn't a dummy!" I was then asked if I realized I was completely exonerated and that I should not go for coffee or have any conversations with anyone who had been in the room. The rest is a blur. I went back to my office and I realized that to keep moving forward I had to accept that this had happened and that whenever I met any of the participants involved, I was to treat them with respect (this was my demand on myself).

Hindsight is a wonderful teacher, and as the years have passed, I realize that, as a leader, there were some barbs of hurt and pain that existed in my heart for a time because of the expectations and assumptions I had made. Those hurts and pain were mine to deal with. I also came to realize that in the hurt and pain, I grappled with an attitude of pride towards my supervisor and others. It was a picture of self-justification, a picture of I had been treated unfairly and I needed to set it right. It was even a picture of I was right, and they were wrong, and I would fix this!

This story from my leadership journey has so many leadership principles worth learning.

The first is the principle of *never blindsiding your leader*, which applies at all levels of leadership. As a contributing person to a joint purpose, leaders and followers should not be blindsided by peers, colleagues, supervisors, or direct reports. This is a simple and yet complex matter of human respect. It is simple in that we can say we are sure we have communicated well and with all involved who need to know. It is complex in that there are so many intertwining issues involved. Leaders are challenged by time, resources, varying people's perspectives, lack of clarity in information, who needs to know, processes, etc. For any project or situation, be sure to take the time to create and put in place clear communication lines and processes. Use them for the benefit of the organizational purpose and work fulfillment of those involved.

The second is the principle of understanding that *ego and/or pride can sometimes be an inside battle and sometimes it is a more obvious outside battle.* As we grow in our own self-awareness, we become aware of the damage unguarded trigger events can have. We also recognize that a lack of understanding of how our emotions can derail us and enable us to make up stories in our heads can produce an environment for us to react in unhealthy ways without understanding the facts. We serve ourselves and the organization well when we learn what is going on inside us and we measure it against what is needed most to move forward in a positive direction. In my story above, in my shock of how the situation was being handled, I had to battle inner ego that wanted to prove how wrong this was and how right I was. It was by self-awareness, reflection, and choosing to stay true to my values that I walked through this situation.

The third is the principle that *there is always more to the story than meets the eye*. No matter where any blame lay in this situation, trust requires that we believe the best of others and also that we are prepared to handle less than the best. This takes extraordinary self-leadership and maturity.

The fourth is the principle of *never burning your bridges because you never know when you will have to walk over them again.* This is so true in leadership. If we choose to carry our hurt and pain, if we refuse to deal with broken relationships, then we build walls rather than bridges to a better future. In the story above, some eleven years later I can say my heart is free to work with that same leadership in a different setting and my heart is free and a whole lot wiser.

The fifth is the principle of *forgiveness*. This is a hard-won battle: to name what happened, to own my part, to make choices that did not feel good in the moment when my heart as a leader was hurting so badly, and yet to work through what it took to forgive. There have been many situations in my life as a leader where I have had to learn to stand true to my values in a spirit of forgiveness if I wanted to be free to move forward.

 Kaleidoscope Reflections

The Giving and Receiving of Forgiveness:

Take time to describe a situation that has left you hurt. Name it, describe it and then work through the following concepts and questions that are most helpful for you. The following are principles to consider:

1. Heart scars take time to heal.

    • Describe the heart scars you are carrying.

    • How are you giving yourself grace to work through them?

2. When a heart starts to trust it is tentative at best.

    • Describe what trust looks like for you in a relationship.

    • Acknowledge in this situation where you felt trust was broken.

    • What is one thing you can do to start to rebuild trust?

3. When something goes off track, trust is broken and taken personally very quickly.

    • How would you describe what went off track?

    • What was your role in this going off track?

    • How did you come to take it personally and what has that done to your heart?

    • What do you want to see change?

4. Conversations based in humility can feel and seem stilted and uncomfortable.

    • How would you describe the way choosing humility makes you uncomfortable?

    • What are the "yeah buts" in your mind around what you have experienced and perceived?

    • Examine them and reflect on how getting stuck in a "yeah but" will limit a trusting relationship.

    • What is one thing you desire to see differently?

5. When we let go of who is right and who is wrong and desire what is right we can give and receive grace.

- Unpack what this statement means to you.

- What does your understanding demand of you?

6. Forgiveness is not just a cheap, "I am sorry."

    - Sorrow over what is not right or good is a step in the direction of the freedom that comes with forgiveness.

    - Describe what other steps you need to take to find freedom in your heart and mind.

7. Forgiveness has to be about the real issue, not just the surface.

    - If you have not already named the real issue, do so now.

    - How ugly is that?

    - Why would you want to deal with the real issue?

    - Are you willing to do that?

8. Forgiveness acknowledges the emotional pain and looks for the facts.

    - Create that healthy conversation in your brain that you read about earlier. Even write the conversation out.

9. Forgiveness says: "Please forgive me I was wrong for _____"

    - Name what your part was in getting to this point.

    - Reflect carefully that there is a genuine ownership of the real issue and not just of wanting to move on and get out of the discomfort of conflict.

10. Forgiveness says: "I forgive you." Forgiveness does not depend on how the other person responds.

    - Free the other person. Let them off your hook of rightness.

11. Forgiveness chooses to let go of the hurt and live with the healing.

    - Forgiveness is a choice that does not necessarily equate with reconciliation.

    - You can long for reconciliation and still be free.

    - You cannot be free without forgiving.

12. Once healing begins, scars can pinch and pull and there may still be some discomfort.

    - Pay attention to the pinches that come. The issue rises up in your mind and your emotions bring it forward with full force.

    - What ways can you acknowledge the pinch?

    - What will you do to get back into a factual space and redirect your emotional energy to serve you in a healthy way?

13. Forgiveness chooses to continue to cleanse the wound and move towards health, rather than nurse

the wound and lean towards protective pride.

- Name and describe the new ways you are more self-aware and others aware as a result of working this situation through in the ways described above.

14. Forgiveness and the process of healing take time.

- Who have you asked to walk with you in this journey? What role are you asking them to play for you to be able to embrace the power of working through criticism and hurt towards a positive end?

15. One day you slowly wake to know the scar has healed and your heart is free once more.

- Reflect and review these teachings.

- How can you turn them into principles of having a healthy outlook on giving and receiving forgiveness?

- In what ways can you raise up **What-if** leaders who know how to face and deal with criticism and the ensuing hurt that it brings?

Many times, we will grapple with criticism and its ensuing hurt. These will be hard times to face and deal within a healthy way in order to find freedom and to be able to move forward. When we refuse or neglect to deal with our hurts, we will find ourselves bleeding, spewing and vomiting on those who have never hurt us. We will lose our leadership edge, our credibility and our influence.

 Kaleidoscope Reflections

Think of and describe a recent leadership situation where you felt the pain of betrayal, hurt, or unfair treatment.

1. How would you describe the expectations you held in that moment? What were the expectations of the situation, of yourself, of others?

2. How would you describe your attitude and behaviour towards the other person(s) in that initial moment of hurt?

3. Reflect on what this meant or looked like for you as a leader in the short term and now in the long term?

4. Describe how carrying hurt towards another, leads to an unhealthy working relationship?

5. What bridges do you sense have been burned, or are in danger of being burnt?

6. What ownership do you need to take so that your heart can be free?

7. What do you value that would empower you to do what is required of you in this situation no matter how it turns out?

8. Describe what having an unhealthy relationship with one of your direct reports looks like

for you as a leader. This is particularly applicable when you have felt slighted, hurt, criticized, or misunderstood by someone at work. How would you describe the stress levels you experience?

9. How could understanding how hurt cripples you, or blinds you to truth, enable you to handle difficult situations and move beyond hurt and its unhealthy aftermath?

Unresolved hurt simmers until it becomes a matter of ego or pride that needs to be protected. Unresolved hurt requires constant thinking about, analyzing and justifying until it becomes bigger in your mind than any possible resolution. Its constant nibbling away at your thoughts diminishes your clarity, your creativity, your ability to discern and move forward. You become stuck.

Pride

Once you are stuck in the need for rightness, you will know that ego has taken hold in a negative way, which we call pride. Letting go of pride allows you to be free to think of other potential right ways, rather than just your own right way. Pride wears many faces and is a part of our human nature, which can diminish, disappoint, defeat, deter, depress, despise, discourage us and make us less than we could possibly be. We have a hard time seeing this in ourselves, and yet it is so easy to pinpoint in others.

The fable of *The Emperor's New Clothes* is a beautiful and clear illustration of the negative power of pride.

The Emperor's New Clothes (Danish: *Kejserens nye klæder*) is a short tale written by Danish author Hans Christian Andersen about two weavers who promise an emperor a new suit of clothes they say is invisible to those who are unfit for their positions, stupid, or incompetent. In reality, they make no clothes at all, making *everyone* believe the clothes are invisible to them. When the emperor parades before his subjects in his new "clothes," no one dares to say they do not see any suit of clothes on him for fear they will be seen as stupid. Finally, a child cries out, "But he isn't wearing anything at all!"

Pride restricts our ability to see and to discern because our focus has shifted to ourselves. Pride will always speak to the awesomeness of oneself above all else and our need to be right.

 Kaleidoscope Reflections

1. Consider the feelings of the faces of pride listed below and circle any of the feelings that you have experienced.

    a. Impatience disdain indifference patronizing better than

    b. Deserving you owe me deprived resentful entitled to

    c. Anxious fearful needy stressed overwhelmed

    d. Helpless jealous bitter depressed not good enough

2. What observations do you make from the exercise you just completed? What is your interpretation of your observations?

3. Describe a situation where you were feeling one of the emotions from one of the faces listed below. Describe how you handled the situation and how it turned out. Are there any observations or learnings for you?

These lists of emotions have names that correlate with a way that expresses pride.

Face 1—I am Superior

We know we are wearing this face when we are impatient with others, frustrated with them, patronizing of them, or just plain disdainful. We exhibit an attitude that we are superior to the other person. We are feeling like we have the right way in the right timing and they just don't get it. It is all about us!

Face 2—I Deserve

We know we are wearing this face when we feel like we are not getting what we deserve from others, or that they owe us, or we are resentful. Again we have become focused on ourselves and what is best for us. It is all about us!

Face 3—I Must Wear a Mask

We know we are wearing this face when we feel anxious, afraid, needy and overwhelmed. We are struggling from wearing a mask and not letting others see who we really are. It is stressful to keep on a game face when everything is falling apart. It is all about us!

Face 4—I am Inadequate

We know we are wearing this face when we feel helpless, bitter, jealous or depressed, or that we simply are not good enough. We are seeing ourselves as inadequate compared to others. It is all about us!

The common denominator with all of these faces that we choose to wear is the focus is all about us. All these ways of seeing ourselves focus on ourselves, limiting our ability to see and comprehend clearly. We cannot see the humanity of others; instead we turn them into objects. This allows us to justify ourselves and the way we see our perspective. This creates a space for us to step into the role of judging others.

What-if we learned to move and act with kindness, with curiosity, by giving the benefit of the doubt and yet being prepared to deal with less than the best? In kindness, could we let go of impatience, disdain, jealousy, fear, or any of the other emotions expressed in the lists above?

Some leaders would consider emotions and feelings something they do not need to deal with. So often I find what is really happening is that there are times we do not recognize our emotions, or we do not have names for them so we assume we do not experience them. Lack of emotional intelligence does not mean we do not experience emotion. It just means we are unaware of ourselves and of others in meaningful ways.

There is a fifth face that allows me to gain perspective in relationship to myself:

We know we are wearing this face when we can view ourselves as having worth and are able to be lifegiving. This allows us to view others as equal in their creation as we are, they are worthy and deserving as people. They deserve to receive rhythms of grace and truth. I recognize that I am wearing this face because I will feel peaceful, optimistically realistic, filled with expectancy, delight, gratitude and   warmth

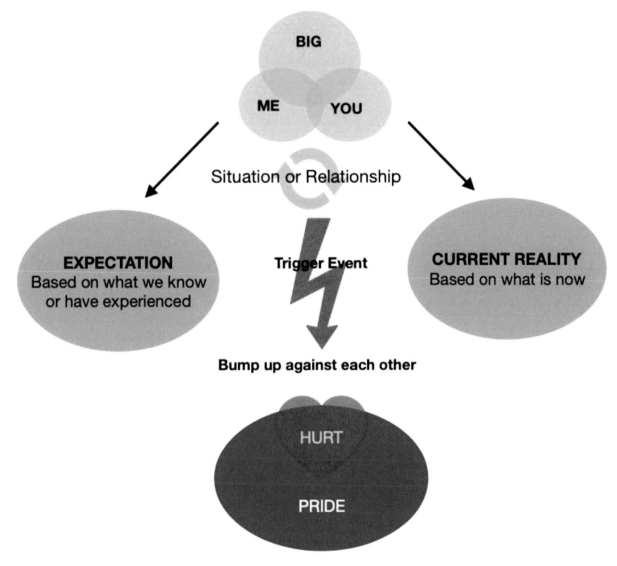

![Kaleidoscope icon] Kaleidoscope Reflections

1. As you consider the feelings and emotions represented in each by each face of pride, is there one face where you tend to land more frequently?

2. In paying attention or becoming more aware of these emotions, what is one thing you can do to shift your mindset when you first recognize this emotional trigger event?

Lack of recognition of our emotions and how they affect us and our relationship with others gives space for our leadership perspective to continue to spiral down. Many would say that pride or ego has a positive side, and yet if the focus is on me then it will eventually break down to too narrow a focus. Confidence would be what I consider a right sized ego. It is aware of one's strengths and abilities and yet can use those strengths and abilities to serve a cause greater than just itself.

3. Describe how you would define the difference between pride or ego and confidence? As you reflect on your behaviours, where do you consider you are displaying pride or ego that is harmful and confidence that will serve to move you forward?

4. Is there a place where you display outward pride or ego because you lack inward confidence? What does that look like and what kind of dissonance does that create inside you?

Idol

An idol is anything that appears bigger than it really is. It elicits emotions that make us believe it is insurmountable and we have become the victim to its strength and power. It controls our emotions, our attitudes and our habits in harmful ways.

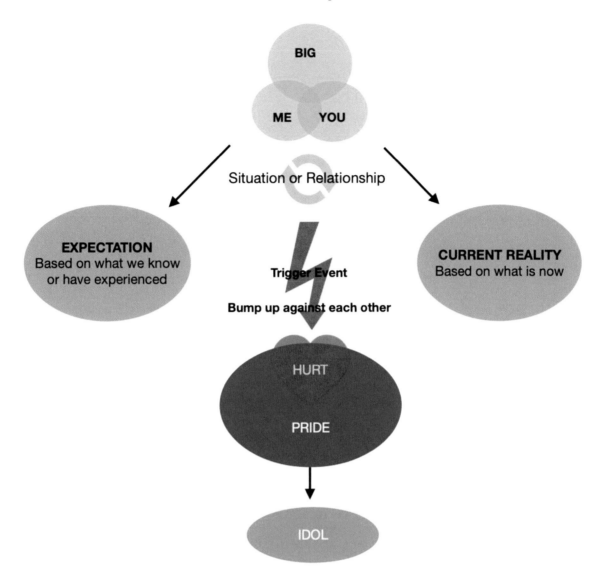

A dear mentor of mine, Jill Briscoe, tells the story of *When the Pig Shows Up!*

Jill Briscoe is an international speaker, who recounts that it doesn't matter where we are or how noble our efforts are, or how prepared we are, the pig will eventually show up. Jill then tells the story of spending her time to prepare to speak, of preparing her heart to deliver it with pure motives, of rising to speak, and the pig shows up. He snorts across her mind with thoughts like, "Wow, look at the size of crowd there is to impress!" Or, "There's so and so; hope they catch my third point!" Or, "I must have a great reputation to speak here." When the pig shows up, we become delusional at the very least and our perspective runs out of control.

We allow the pig to roll in the mud, we bathe him, we dress him up, we put a bow on his ear. The pig is a metaphor for our thoughts. We do the same thing with our thoughts. In other words, we can cater to our thoughts even when we know they are out of line. The pig rules! We make his piggishness bigger than reality. The result is that drama ensues within and it can also ensue with others. Our other choice is to leave the pig in the pigpen and walk away.

Kaleidoscope Reflections

1. What is a pig situation for you—that is, where everything becomes bigger than is true and it affects how you view the situation or relationship? You have perhaps dramatized and made up stories in your head about the situation and/or the person involved that may or may not be true and yet those stories hold you stuck.

2. As you think about this stuck relationship from a different angle, what are you learning about yourself, about the situation, about what you realize you do not know to be true?

Our piggishness when we refuse to STOP- REFLECT- RECALCULATE leads to conflict.

Conflict

When we become fixated on a difficult relationship, we see our way as right and the only way. When everything to do with us becomes bigger than reality, we then find ourselves losing sleep over it. We fear seeing or meeting that person. We begin to feel that there is nothing we can do to make it better. We find a dissonance within which spills over into conflict with others.

We are stuck. We are stuck in pride. If we go back to the feelings in those lists, we will see how pride is negatively influencing our opinion, our way of being, and our behaviours.

We can find a lot of material that speaks to conflict resolution from the outside. An understanding of our pride will give us an understanding of how our way of seeing things through the lens of pride hinders us and gets us stuck. We even bring conflict into the room with us when we are stuck in pride.

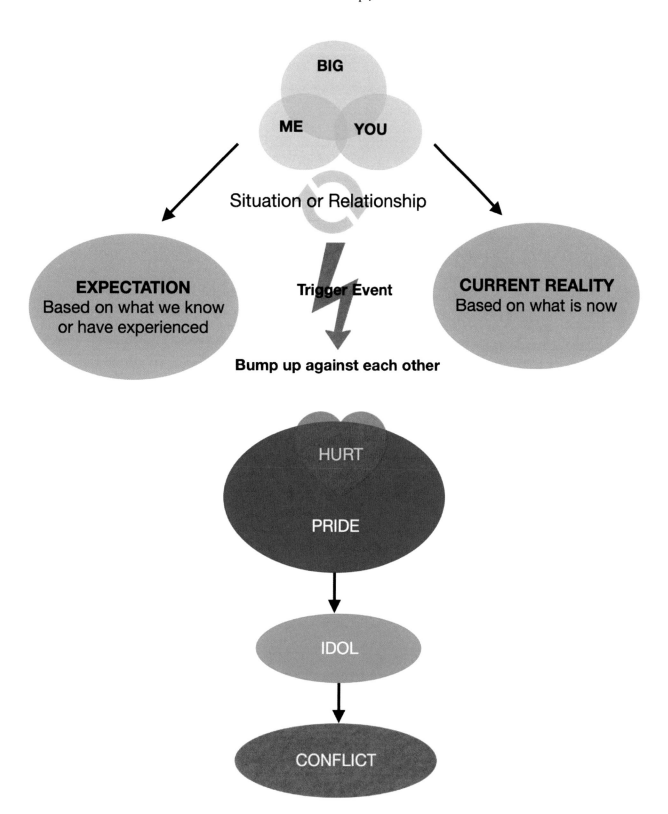

What-if you found a way to work through conflict that made you a better leader, a more integrated leader?

Having a healthy view of yourself, of what is the BIG in your life, of how others are equal in their creation just as you are, will help to redefine the whole concept of conflict for you as a leader. It helps us to realize we all are human; we all have perspectives that may or may not jive. We all bring differences to the table that can collectively make us more.

Whenever you face a difference in yourself and another person, the potential for conflict is there. For example, if I am female and you are male, there will be some inherent differences.

If I am Scottish and you are another nationality, there will be potential for differences.

If I am poor and you are rich, or vice versa, there is potential for differences.

If I am of one faith and you are of another there is a potential for differences.

If I am older than you there is potential for differences.

And the list for potential differences continues and is long. We can be fixated on what draws us apart or focus on how to maximize those differences and then draw together for the sake of unity. Unity is not uniformity; it is the bringing together of all that is different to work as a cohesive whole.

There are times as a leader I wonder, **What-if** our real job is to navigate all the differences and bring honour and respect to the conversation that will bring the best out in everyone? There are times I have thought that this is perhaps one of the "unspoken family rules" of leadership. I have come to ask myself in the light of differences:

What-if we were created this way so we were given the opportunity to learn to play together well in the sandbox?

Or

What-if we were created this way in order to learn how to honour one another, to respect the strengths and abilities each one brings to the table?

Detailed reflection was given in the section on **Hurt**. If you didn't complete it, I encourage you to go back and spend some time there.

 Kaleidoscope Reflections

1. When you think back over a challenging relationship where you just wanted to avoid that person, try describing what had been happening prior to this.

2. What were you feeling and/or sensing?

3. What did you know for sure?

4. Describe how you experience dissonance on the inside.

5. How might that dissonance be an early warning signal that something within is out of line?

6. Describe your patterns of conflict.

7. How could you build on your differences to make a more integrated whole?

There is a powerful saying I use in my leadership world: Gradually, then suddenly! This is a quote from Ernest Hemingway who was asked, "How did you go broke?" Hemingway's answer was, "Gradually, then suddenly." So often it seems like relationships get turned off suddenly, and yet when you stop to look back at the timeline of events, you will see it was one uncared for situation there and another one here. Pretty soon all the here's and there's add up to a whole lot of stressful situations compounded by a lack of emotional responses, poor communication and unhealthy dialogue. Discovering our patterns of conflict frees us to recognize the negative power of conflict that diminishes our credibility as a leader.

Over my years as a leader, I came to recognize that there was one particular personality that I would tend to bump up against. As I became more aware of personality conflicts, I also learned to focus on what the BIG was that drove me. Knowing and understanding who I am and who the other person is, freed me to be authentic and to handle conflict with confidence. Conflict is a part of life; it stops us in our tracks. We have the choice to make changes to harness its power in order to fulfill our calling and/or our purpose. Conflict will always take work and emotional energy to move through. Recognizing our patterns and having some tools to handle conflict eases the way in the midst of hard relational work.

For example, as a young leader I assumed I needed to have the answer as soon as I was asked. I often stressed over, "What if I don't have the 'right' answer?" One of the principles that came to serve me well is one I call buying time. It meant I didn't have to go through the stress of wearing a mask, which was all about "I got this" or "I am right." I came to understand that when faced with something I was uncertain about or I didn't know, I could have healthy responses tucked away that bought me time and allowed for clear and informed conversations. Some responses I learned to use when I felt a trigger event, or when I felt uncertain, or when I didn't know the answer were:

Hmmm, I appreciate what you just told me. I appreciate having a little time to think about that and I will get back to you.

Or

Wow! I wasn't aware of all that, or of the whole story. Let me take some time to process it and get back to you.

Or

Hmmm, I obviously have not had all the information. Let me give this some consideration and get back to you.

Or

Wow! I really don't know, let me get back to you.

Try using the above concepts and find the language that is true to who you are. If you are given information that you should have known and you don't know, take responsibility for your lack of knowing with honesty. For example, "I think I should have known that, and I don't. Please let me get back to you." This is not a tool for manipulation. This is a tool to take ownership and find a way to address it honestly. If you say you need time and will get back to them, then do just that. Our inability to learn to handle our internal and external conflicts will lead us to isolate ourselves. It will cause us to withdraw from others and from situations where we are called on to interact with others.

Isolation

When a disease is rampant, isolation is a good thing. In order to contain an infectious disease, isolation would be considered a part of a healthy treatment to stop the spread of the disease.

Social isolation differs from loneliness in that loneliness is a temporary separation or sense of little connection with other people. We can be lonely and be in a crowd of people. It is an inner sense of not being seen or heard, or of feeling we are of little importance and so there is no real connection with others in the moment. Isolation can appear similar and yet can go further than loneliness. It is a willful withdrawing of oneself from meaningful contact with others.

Isolation becomes a result of unhealthy, unresolved conflict either internal or external. The focus becomes on oneself and the sense of unworthiness, even shame and not sensing a place of belonging with others. It can come from a sense of being the only one with the right answer and being unwilling to even look at where one might possibly be mistaken. It is a choice to dull the dissonance of unresolved conflict by avoidance and/or distraction. All these come from the lists we described as being pride.

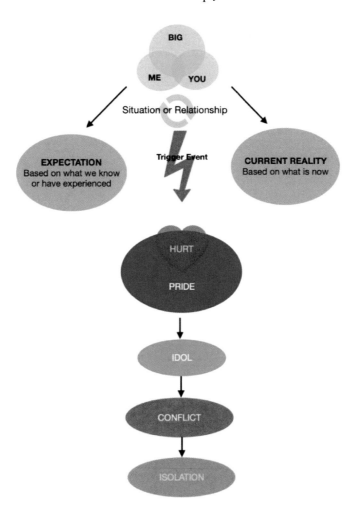

In the story told earlier about when I appeared before the grievance committee, the thoughts crossed my mind in the aftermath of the meeting to quit, to give up, to walk away. Those thoughts were fleeting because of many healthier influences, which we will talk about in the next chapter in How to Get Unstuck.

 Kaleidoscope Reflections

1. As a leader, where are you turning a blind eye to unhealthy relationships that create dissonance for you and tempt you to avoid the downside of unresolved conflict?

2. Be clear and honest about how conflict in relationships has caused you to become jaded or even bitter.

3. Take the time to reflect and write out the scenario as it unfolded and consider one thing you need to do to begin to be resonant or at peace inside again.

When we choose isolation over healthy introspection and both outer and inner accountability, we then find ourselves stuck in self-destruction.

Self-destruction

As we follow this pathway, we begin to recognize what a downward spiral it is when we hold a casual disregard for the healthy **What-ifs** of leadership.

Self-destruction can come to us in many ways. We can get stuck in the space of:

- doubting our worth

- doubting we have skills and abilities

- doubting our relationships

- doubting we have a place of belonging in our family, in our workplace, or in our world

- doubting that what we have is not worth preserving

- doubting that our life has worth

At any point in time we can lose our way by the current reality of life circumstances we find ourselves a part of. We can get lost in the pain, the emotions, the circumstances, the unhealthy relationships. As I have shared this concept, time and again I have heard people say, "That is me! I don't know who I am any more, and I don't feel like I have anything of value to offer." These people have been highly functioning leaders who have gotten stuck somewhere along this downward spiral and had lost hope. The harder they tried, the less they felt they had anything of value to offer.

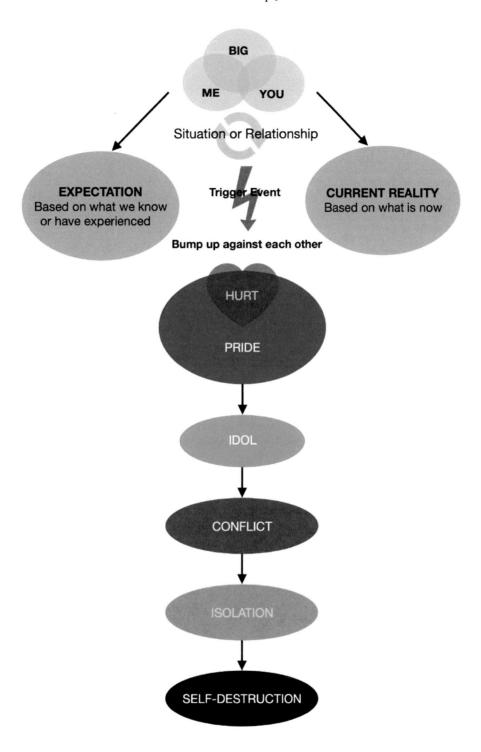

During the early years of being a highly valued volunteer leader, I remember the darkness of personal loss that changed my life. It seemed like overnight and yet it was not. I began to spiral down, first because of life circumstances and then by unrealistic and hurtful expectations put on me by leadership. I was a young mom, a new mom, and in the course of one year I lost my mom to cancer within six weeks of diagnosis; I lost my aunt to death by a drunk driver; I lost another young family member to suicide. I was devastated and reeling emotionally, physically, relationally, in about every way you can name. I had not travelled this road before.

I was overcome by the darkness of postnatal depression, the darkness of grief and mourning. I was lost. I was to fear-filled and fear-driven, convinced each morning that I would lose one of my children or that my husband would be taken from me. I was wrapped in emotional chains that bound my head and heart and revealed only darkness and hopelessness to me. I was nauseated, anxious, undone. Little did I know that the next nine years would hold more of the same losses, including financial loss. As these losses took their toll on my confidence and ability to step out into former leadership roles, I also experienced pressure from some to get over it and to get involved again. I wish it had been that simple and that easy. It was a long, hard journey of letting others in, of facing my demons, of choosing to learn how to train my mind with new neural pathways that weren't so wrapped up in negativity, defeat and fear.

I am grateful to say that from my present vantage point I recognize that through the grace of God I found hope, I was given tools, I was blessed with relationships that would not let me go. I fought, I persevered, I made choices from desperation and slowly—oh so slowly—I saw light again. I felt a sense of joy bubbling up through a whole new world that I had not known. I experienced the stop in the midst of the downward spiral. I gained a greater empathy for others whose lives were turned upside down. I learned to hear them, to walk with them, to nudge them to make healthy choices and to use their minds and hearts to rise above guilt and a victim mentality.

The commentary is sad for the life that knows the tasks, understands the processes and yet has neglected their own growth and transformation along the way. They have neglected, or even ceased to allow, the pain and hurt of the reality of life to shape and mold them into a greater person. They have given in to the lie that pushing through will solve it all. They burn out. They find satisfaction in lesser things. They lose their way. We see the leaders who begin or at some point recognize their purpose. They are out of the starting gate with great gusto and yet somewhere they cease to become. So, they never reach the place of life recognition and we then wonder where they have gone. Whatever happened to _____? In self-destruction we have come to a place where we have lost our way and the purpose we were given when placed on this earth. Our hope has been lost. We have not found what can hold us through the deep, dark days of pain, loss and depression.

It seems that our life circumstances become the victor. We only see the dark of what we never wanted and fail to grasp even a tiny possibility of our far greater potential. If we do what it takes for us to admit where we are—to grow in resiliency, to push through the hard and discouraging times, and to grab one bit of life at a time—then there is a new beginning. This is no sugar-coated journey. This is the journey of bloody battles fought, of death staring us in the face, of hopelessness wrapping us in cold, hard chains. There are times as we do this journey when we do get stuck a little, or stuck a whole lot, where we no longer recognize the person we were or could yet be. All along this downward spiral there are stopping points, places of grace to see differently, to think differently, to act differently.

I believe they are the **What-if** moments of life and leadership.

These moments of doubt, darkness, and desperation come to all of us as leaders in different ways, times and spaces. They are the spaces we would never choose. They are the dark night of the leadership soul. They also are the moments of redefining and reframing ourselves as leaders and our leadership.

We might describe them as the Infinity Loop of Leadership.

The Infinity Loop of Leadership explains that we were created or born with a purpose beyond ourselves, integrating our passion and purpose, finding and deepening meaningful relationships, choosing inner and outer accountability and living with a full out spirit of gratitude that produces a life focused on reflection. As this all creates a rhythm in our life and leadership we recognize when we need to address change and transition before we self-destruct.

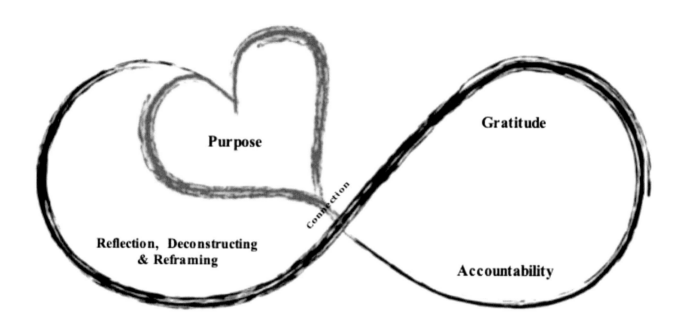

Purpose

Gratitude

Connection

Reflection, Deconstructing & Reframing

Accountability

Kaleidoscope Reflection

1. Purpose is the BIG that is greater than you and drives who you are, what you do and influences the choices you make.

   Describe your purpose.

2. Connection is where your experience, your passion and purpose come together. How would you describe your passion that is in line with your purpose?

   What is a metaphor or simile for your passion?

   It is finding and deepening those relationships that sustain and move you forward. Name who these relationships are for you.

3. Accountability is both the intrinsic and extrinsic values and processes that keep you

pursuing your purpose.

Name the accountabilities you have in place that celebrate who you are and what you do, as well as what challenges you in who you are and what you do.

4. Gratitude is a way of being with a capital G.

How are you developing an outlook of gratitude in every season and nuance of your leadership journey?

5 Reflection—these are your unguarded moments of intentionality, of sitting back on the balcony or the window seat (you will learn more about these in Life Management). Here you consider your life and leadership from the perspective of what you say is the BIG in your life and from the bigger picture.

You have named your BIG. What is creating dissonance for you? Describe the resonance you sense with your BIG?

6. Deconstruct is where you make decisions around questions like, what is going well? What is not going well? What do I keep, and why does that matter? What do I celebrate and let go of, and why does that matter?

7. Reframe is about taking a fresh look, adding to it what is left, what you see could be, and defining the new dream that is possible before the present one collapses and/or dies.

What do you have left to build on and bring continuity? What are you seeing that could possibly be?

How would you describe this new dream for yourself as a leader, or for the organization?

The above exercise is a simpler version of what you will find in **Section 2**: *Integration,* where you will take a deep dive into who you are as a leader and how you are choosing to lead and to grow.

First let's consider how we can get unstuck.

Notes—record your most significant thoughts to reflect on and to begin bold action.

_____

_____

_____

_____

_____

_____

_____

_____

_____

_____

_____

_____

_____

_____

_____

_____

_____

_____

_____

Chapter 3

What Gets Us Unstuck

Values

Values are living with healthy confidence and dealing with pride, building unity out of diversity, getting rid of unhealthy messages where we look for sameness rather than look for wholeness or completeness.

What-if being stuck was preparation for us to rise to greater effectiveness as leaders?

For those of us who are driven and purposeful, there are times it is even hard to imagine we could ever get stuck, and then there are times when life and leadership catch us by surprise and throw us off. We flounder and do not recognize ourselves. This is not us! We may ponder, we may wallow, we may think of walking away and yet we look for something different, we look for spaces to be regrouped and to once again become.

For my leadership journey, one of the greatest gifts to me was discovering the power of a values inspired life. As I walked this journey of discovery, I found it was one that was hard, it was inspiring, it was constant, and it yielded great rewards. My conscious journey in discovering the value inspired life all began with just one word, INSPIRE! It was a word that was in living colour to me.

Sometime after my decade of loss, grief and mourning, I remember when the tiny glimpses of sunlight began to appear at the end of the tunnel. One of my losses had been my Uncle Ross.

When Uncle Ross passed away from an unknown lung disease, my Auntie Dorothy sold us their old and well-loved camper van. It was a beast to drive and yet it was a wonderful gift. It provided many solitary and also family getaways to the mountains. I was able to head to the mountains where the very sight of them fed my soul and created space for reflection, processing and moving forward.

One of these great times came when my eldest daughter, Melodie and I decided to go on a weekend camping trip to Banff National Park. I felt like a hardy truck driver behind the wheel of this loose steering rig! Not that I enjoyed that feeling, but the van got us where we were going!

I digress to say that I had come to recognize what I felt was a rare gift I had been given and that was to see in metaphors and pictures. I can remember listening to people and there in my mind would be a picture version of what they were saying. I was often laughed at (lovingly, I am sure) and mocked (with the best of heart) for these pictures I also had the audacity to share with others! Those pictures made me sit up and pay attention. What did this mean and why did it matter?

At this time, I had been serving on staff as a part of the senior leadership team at a large church in Calgary as Pastor of Life Transformation. The role was so fulfilling and a new page of my life. Early one morning, while Melodie and I were camping, Melodie was still sleeping. I got up and made some coffee and walked down to the river to enjoy the early morning quiet and to journal.

Here is an excerpt from the journal.

> *"As I sat and watched the sun rise, I saw a dark gray shale mountain face transformed by golden sunlight. It caught my attention and gave me pause for thought."*

In that moment I remember sensing that I was at a turning point. I had been given a new opportunity to see things differently, to see the opportunity before me, to use my skills and abilities in a new setting. I could learn more about my leadership, the leadership the organization needed and how those could fit together. There was a newness, a freshness, an opportunity to move out of dark spaces into light. I began to affirm through times of reflection what I truly valued in life, and it began with one simple word that I referred to earlier: INSPIRE. In chapter one, I told a brief rendition of how and when I discovered the word INSPIRE in a new and fresh way.

As we consider the template from chapter one, where do values fit in to your life and leadership?

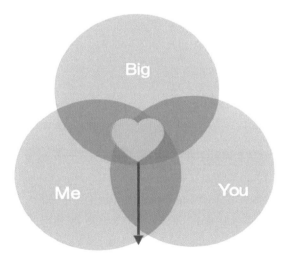

Our **perspectives** when drawn together by our
values and what we have in common.

Values fit in the small space where the three circles intersect. There are organizational values, personal values and the values of others. When a trigger event occurs, if we have clarity on our values, we can stop right there and consider what conversations are needed, when they are needed, and with whom to come to a collaborative position for all. If hurt occurs before that conversation happens, then there is additional conversation needed around the situation. This continues down the spiral. At any point we can:

STOP-REFLECT- RECALCULATE

As we think of the places we get stuck, I want to move us in the direction of understanding some exercises and processes to define and embrace our values and allow them to make us even more than we are today.

> More integrated
> More effective
> More peace-filled
> More capable
> More in tune with ourselves and with others
> More purposeful

Do you know what your values are?

Do you know how your values can reveal your hot buttons that lead to emotional reactions? Do you know how your values can be a source of accountability for living and being all you were created to be as a leader?

Do you know how you can use your values to resolve conflicts in a powerful and deeply meaningful way?

Do you know how you can use your values to lead a team in the same direction in spite of individual differences?

We have values:

> That we aspire to;
> That we live by, whether we can name them or not;
> That are intrinsic to us, they resonate deep within us;
> That are extrinsic to us, they are influenced by others' expectations of us.

Getting to the Heart of the Matter

This article by Richard Eckersley speaks to the fundamental breakdown in our culture and ultimately to the breakdown of values.

> *"The modern scourges of Western civilization, such as youth suicide, drug abuse, and crime, are usually explained as personal, social, and economic terms: unemployment, poverty, child abuse, family breakdown, and so on.*
>
> *And yet my own research suggests the trends appear to be, at least to some extent, independent of such factors. They seem to reflect something more fundamental in the nature of Western societies.*
>
> *I believe this "something" is a profound and growing failure of Western culture—a failure to provide a*

sense of meaning, belonging, and purpose in our lives as well as a framework of values.

People need to have something to believe in and live for. They need to feel they are part of a community and a valued member of society, and they need to have a sense of spiritual fulfillment. That is, they need a sense of relatedness and connectedness to the world and the universe in which they exist."

 Kaleidoscope Reflection

1. As you read this article what did you resonate with in the article from your leadership perspective?

2. How do you understand that this concept may be at work in your organization?

3. What comes to mind as ways to shift this thinking?

Actions will always reveal what people believe.

4. Ask yourself the question: How does what I am doing right now reveal what I believe?

The way we choose to think and behave truly reveals what we value or what is most important to us. When the values we hold get stepped on, it creates emotional responses, which may or may not serve us well. In survival, gut instinct based on our values is crucial. In building healthy organizations and relationships our gut needs to be at times tempered and guided by values that inspire us and move us forward.

There are a number of ways we can determine what we value in word and also in our behaviours. We will explore some of those exercises as we work through this chapter. There are times we hold values for others and we neglect to see that we are not living by that value.

I grew up in a home where the values of consistency and integrity were important. This may seem like a simplistic story and yet it has impacted me all my adult life.

As a little girl, I learned to bake and cook with my mom. When we made chocolate chip cookies, I would want to eat the dough! Mom would say, "No, we make the dough and bake the cookies for others." I did get to lick the bowl when I helped bake! When Mom said no to me she also lived by that no. When I grew up and started teaching my children to bake, I finally realized when I wanted something as an adult it was very easy to expect my children to obey and yet for me to choose what I wanted for myself. My childhood story often came back and gave me the courage to live the same way I expected my children to live.

I call this story the Cookie Principle in Leadership: "Don't expect from others what you are not willing to do yourself!" Many times, I have heard leaders give expectations for their people and do the opposite themselves, which at times has led to secrecy and the need to wear a mask. Our values give us a base, an accountability measure for living what we say.

The following is an extensive exercise for naming, defining and seeing our lives; an opportunity to pay attention to what we say and to see the gap in what we do or don't do.

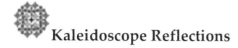

Kaleidoscope Reflections

Calendar, Credit Card Values Test

Sometimes the values we think we embrace are actually different from those we live. We may discover that some outside influence, such as family, religion, or employer, has a value priority that they think we should have, but it is not really a strong value for us. We call these ideal values that are extrinsic to us, rather than actual values that are intrinsic to us. One way to determine your actual values is to apply the calendar and credit card values test.

Let's start by looking at how you are actually living your values right now. Take out your calendar and a credit card statement.

Go through your calendar and record on the chart that follows what activities you did for the last two weeks or months and beside each activity record what value that represents. Ask yourself, "Why did it matter that I did that?" Be sure to also consider your non-calendar activities such as sleep, eating, preparing to eat, appointments, social media time and TV time which probably do not appear on your calendar.

Take a moment to reflect on what values you see reflected in your actual living activities. Comment on which ones resonate with you and which ones you are questioning.

Now complete the same exercise with your credit card and/or debit card transactions. What did you spend your money on and why did each expenditure matter? What values do you see revealed? What has surprised you and what made you say yes?

What's Next?

To apply the calendar and credit card test, look at each of the values listed above and ask yourself, "How much time do I spend each week trying to acquire or increase this value?"

If you feel comfortable with the amount of time you devote to building that value into your life, place a plus mark (+) in the appropriate column; if not, give it a minus (-). After completing the time column, continue in the same way with the money column, making a plus mark if you are satisfied and a minus mark if you are dissatisfied with the amount of money you spend trying to acquire or increase this value.

Note: This exercise may be difficult for some of the more intangible values, such as integrity, but do your best to complete it. Ask yourself, for example: "Have I spent the time or money necessary to meet a promise I've made?" Or, "How is this value showing up in my everyday life?" Or, "Am I satisfied with how I am living this value?"

Knowing your values allows you to make wise and solid decisions based on your deep inner convictions and beliefs.

Activity or Expense	Why does it matter? Name the Value.	Do I live this value consistently? + tYes - No	What is one thing I can do to be more consistent in living this value?

Once you have completed this values chart:

As you reflect on your top values you may notice that one or more of them appear to be a stark contrast to another value. List any of your top values that might conflict with each other (for example, adventure and stability). Explore what the conflict might be. Understand that often your choices are not between good and poor values, but between two really great values. These decisions are hard to make.

Intrinsic Challenges

1. Write down the ways this may explain any intrinsic conflict.

2. How can you address this dilemma in seeking to live by your values?

Extrinsic Challenges

1. Think about relationships you have with superiors, direct reports. Prepare yourself to have a conversation around what they value, what you value and where there are values that bump up against each other.

2. Decide together how you can communicate around what your rules of engagement will be when you agree on your values and more importantly when you disagree.

3. In the conversation, discuss how these values that may be similar, or they may be different, affect your personal relationships or your working relationships. What can you do to capitalize on the similarities and to respect and honour the differences? Discuss and write down several action ideas for an enhanced personal or working relationship.

4. Consider whether your job fits your values and what atmosphere will best harmonize with your values. List any actions you can take to minimize any workplace values conflicts or to change your job or environment to be more compatible with your personal values.

Integrity Based Process for Values Inspired Living

The following chart is simply a visual to explain how our values affect who we are and what we do.

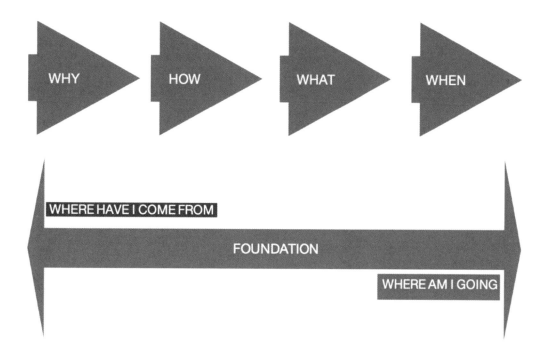

Foundations

Each of our lives is based on a set of beliefs or principles that we have built over a lifetime. Our upbringing has had a profound effect on how we see the world and how we react or respond to what we see. For me personally, my life has been molded and built on the Christian ethic as expressed in the Bible. It has given me a clear picture of truth, of what makes for a rich and fulfilling life. It gives me principles to follow and pitfalls to avoid. Your foundation may be different. Clarify the foundation you want to build your life upon.

Why is about our values:

• Everything we think
• Every decision we make
• Every attitude we carry
• Every behaviour we display

All of these have a 'why' behind them.

WHY

Kouzes and Posner in their leadership classic *The Leadership Challenge* speak of the way values influence our lives.

"Values influence every aspect of our lives: our moral judgments, our responses to others, our commitment to personal and organizational goals. Values set the parameters for the hundreds of decisions we make every day. Options that run counter to our value system are seldom acted upon; and if they are it's done with a sense of compliance rather than commitment. Values constitute with our 'bottom line'"

- Values serve as guides to action
- Values serve to empower
- Values serve to motivate and inspire

To live a life of integrity we must know ourselves and the things we deeply care about. As we see those converge in our lives, we take on a view of leadership that is compelling and inspiring to ourselves and others. Leaders who base decisions on their values and the values of the organization demonstrate and require integrity.

WHAT is about Our Strategic Intentions

The **WHAT** is the big picture of our lives, the things we want to accomplish.

- Our educational choices
- Our retirement plans
- The home we desire
- Our family
- Our service
- Our finances, etc.

Example:

I feel a discontent inside, a dissonance about my career. As I examine that discontent, I find I am moving towards taking further education. This goal of education will drive decisions around my finances, where we live, what school I choose, how I manage my time, my family, etc. This explains how we often create space for trigger events by our lack of paying attention or thinking things through. One decision often sets off the domino effect of a myriad of little decisions that can create resistance in others when we neglect to be aware and honour their values as well.

The **WHAT** of our values is where we will often differ. We may have the same values as someone else, but how we live them out may look different.

For example, I may hold the value of communication. The way I love to communicate most is face-to-face, be that in person or on screen where we can see and experience more than words that are heard. My least favourite is email or text. So, when someone I work with only wants to email, I may struggle with this. Defining what is meaningful communication is important for reducing potential conflicts.

- Difficult and also affirming conversations are for face-to-face space.
- Information is for email—these are the facts.
- Text is for quick check ins.

When we lose sight of these definitions and use these forms of communication in ineffective ways, we create more negative energy and hinder moving forward in a positive way.

HOW is about our bite-size steps of the work.

Bite-size pieces of work are the manageable pieces of how we will accomplish our strategic intentions.

Example:

Strategic Intention—Further education in (field of choice). Bite-size steps of the work:

- Percent of paycheck towards education costs.
- Loans, if needed.
- Explore educational institutes that offer courses and/or degrees in the field of choice.
- How I will manage what activities I do or don't do as I put education as a priority in my life.
- Other.

WHEN is about our commitment to get it on the calendar

When is complex to understand. It is about timing, meeting deadlines, allowing time for prep as well as the actual activity we think is important. **When** is often neglected and creates a physical opportunity for burnout. These are the daily, weekly, and monthly tasks that must show up on my calendar for me to be successful at accomplishing this goal.

Values keep us inspired and focused to be all we can be and to do all we were created to do. This is about being a person of integrity and living a life that is integrated. What we value is what shows up on our calendar and what we actually do, not just what we say.

Example:

For me, the strategic intention of further education is broken down into a number of manageable steps of work. One of the steps of work is to visit certain educational institutions that have expertise in my field of interest. The next step would be to contact these institutions and make an appointment to see a number of people who could give me information for my future direction and decision. These dates will go on my calendar so they will actually happen.

One of the reflective exercises you completed was the calendar/credit card exercise. You began to see what you consider to be your values. Some are intrinsic to you and others are extrinsic.

You probably discovered that you may say you hold some values, which in reality are not reflected in your life or leadership.

It is worthy to note that there are so many values it would be impossible to live by every value we can name or even say is important to us. It becomes important to narrow the values of greater importance to us so that we can truly live and lead with integrity. As Dr. Henry Cloud would say it is about having "the courage to meet the demands of reality."

A helpful exercise is to use the *Values Inspired Living Cards* to name, define and seek to embrace up to ten of our top values in an intentional way in your life.

Values Template

This exercise is one that can help you think through in a logical and meaningful way what you consider your top ten values to be.

Take out your Values Cards.(see Resource Page)

Remove the blank ones. This pack holds about forty-five values cards and definitions. As you complete this exercise you will realize there are many more values than are represented on the cards. You may have value that is not on a card. Use the one of the blank cards to write that value and its definition.

As you flip through the cards you are going to create three piles that represent what values you want to intentionally focus on.

PILE ONE—those values that you know are most important to you.
PILE TWO—those values that you consider important and yet are not sure if they are in your top ten.
PILE THREE—those values you may be living, but you know are not in your top ten for importance.

It is humanly impossible to focus on more than ten values at a time and that could even be a stretch.

This exercise is about the values you are going to intentionally pursue at developing and living out more fully at this time. You probably are living out many more values. Don't quit living them but don't worry about them; just choose the ones you want to focus on right now.

Once you have chosen a maximum of ten, then make two piles.

PILE ONE—Place your top three values.
PILE TWO—Place your other seven values.

Once you have chosen your top three, choose one of those three to be your top value and place the other two on the pile of seven.

Now place these values on the following chart. This is simply a visual for memory purposes.

My Present Values

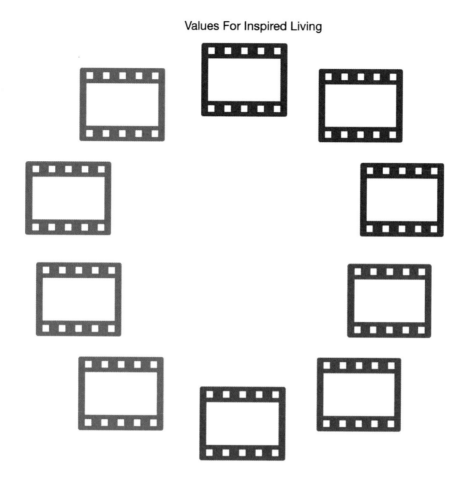

Values For Inspired Living

Example:

I have eight values that I seek to intentionally live out, but one of them, when I focus on it, seems to make it easier or much more possible to live out the other seven. It really expresses strong passion and understanding for me. If I only had one value, this one would give me a strong guide to live a life of integrity. I use this one value as a measuring stick for how I have lived my day and it governs my actions and interactions, my responses and reactions. It also governs what I need to do when I get off track. There may be one like that for you.

So my top values (not in any order) are inspiring, creative, intentional, reflective, God-centered, people-oriented, curious, and courageous. When I first began this process of intentionally naming and defining my values, I had a few others on the list until I was able to identify the ones that truly were intrinsic to me.

The one that underlies them all is "Inspiring." As a result of my faith-based foundation, which has served me well over a lifetime, I define inspiring as, "I am taking the time to allow God to breathe His very life into me, and I then in turn have something of worth that is bigger than myself to breathe out on others."

In order to have leadership integrity, when I come to the end of a day I ask myself:

1. Was I inspiring today?

   a. If the answer is yes, then what did that look like in who I was and what I did? Who else deserves the credit for what I accomplished in an inspiring way? Give that credit to where it is due.

   b. If the answer was no, then I have to do the hard work of looking at my reactions, own them, forgive myself for what was wrong and go and make it right with whoever I wronged.

This is the hard and fulfilling work of living by my values. I could ask those questions of any of my values and yet my value of inspiring, when effective, seems to line up all the other values as well.

In order to fully embrace and live out your values you need to understand them. The following exercise will enable you to know how to recognize when you are living by your values and when you are not. For me this exercise brought my values alive and enabled me to see how integrated I was as a leader. As I saw what my gaps or blind spots were, I could address them.

I think you are beginning to realize that being a leader is not just a role or a set of expectations on the job. It is the hard work of growing and becoming all you can be for a purpose greater than yourself.

 Kaleidoscope Reflection

Values Definition Template

These questions will aid you in developing your understanding of the values you have chosen and what they could look like in your life. Use a journal to record the work you are doing here or complete the work on your computer. Choose your top value to work through this template and then thoughtfully work all your values through the template.

1. **Value**: name of the value.

2. **Definition**: look up the definition in the dictionary or craft a definition that is most meaningful to you and resonates with who you are.

3. **Opposite:** Use your dictionary or thesaurus to determine what the opposite of that value would look like.

4. **Quotes:** What quotes can you find that inspire you about this value? They may be from any place including the newspaper, books you are reading, magazines, etc.

5. **What:** What do you want to accomplish by having this value? This is the STRATEGIC INTENTION.

6. How: How do you want to live this value to accomplish your STRATEGIC INTENTION? What are your STEPS?

7. **When:** Where does this value fit on your CALENDAR? It will be in the form of the tasks to complete the steps that accomplish the STRATEGIC INTENTION.

8. What would hinder you from living this value? What can you do about this?

9. What resources do you already have in place, and what resources do you need to seek to acquire?

10. What changes do you need to make in the way you live and when will you do that?

 Kaleidoscope Reflection

Now that you have named and defined up to ten of your top values, fill in the blank integrity process chart in order to get the feel for how your values truly can influence and enrich your life and leadership.

Briefly state what FOUNDATION (your philosophy of life or your world view) you want to build your life upon.

Choose one VALUE (the why) to follow through on.

State one STRATEGIC INTENTION (the what) you want to accomplish by having this VALUE. State up to three steps (the how) for how you will accomplish that STRATEGIC INTENTION.

Define and place your steps in relation to this STRATEGIC INTENTION on your CALENDAR (the when).

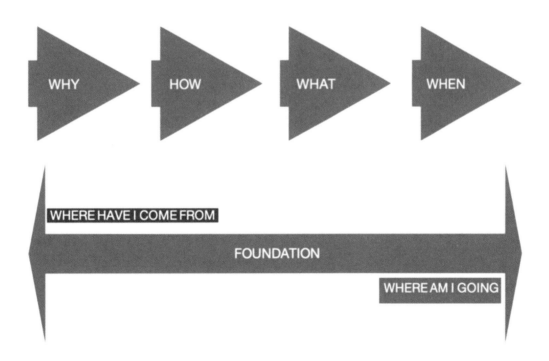

Kaleidoscope Reflection

1. What deeper understanding have you come to, in regards to Values-Based Living?

2. What one thing can you do to apply this knowledge?

3. Where will that fit on your calendar?

Values Effectiveness Template

In the section on Transformation, we will discuss life leadership in greater depth. One part of life leadership is reflecting on how your values are being lived out.

The following template gives you a reflective tool to contemplate how you are doing in living out your values in reality. To add to its effectiveness fill it out yourself, and then ask a supervisor, or direct report, or a peer to fill it out on what they see in you. Then begin to instigate a conversation with them based on two questions to start:

1. What do you see going well in my leadership that you want to celebrate?

2. What do you want to caution me about in my leadership?

Then you can take this information to measure against what you see and know about yourself and where you may possibly have to make adjustments. All of us have gaps, blind spots, or "we do not know what we do not know!" These kinds of focused conversations can give us so much great space to grow and continue to develop in our leadership, no matter where we are on the leadership journey.

On a previous chart (My Present Values) you have listed up to ten of your current values. Place each of these values on the chart that follows.

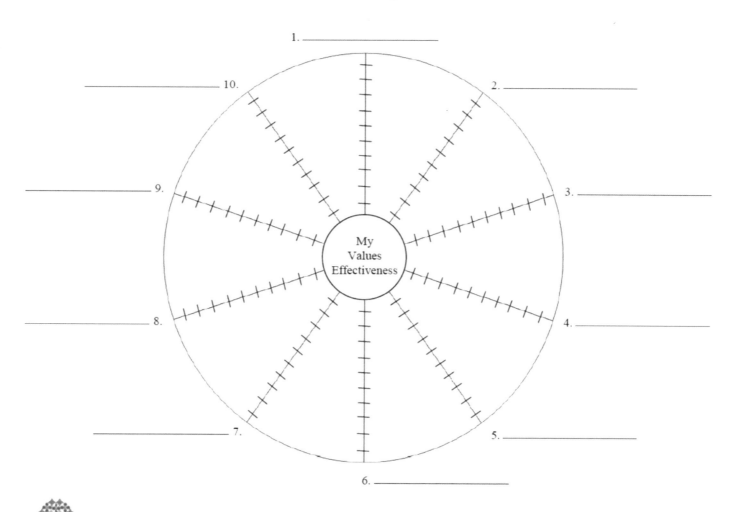

1. _____

10. _____

2. _____

9. _____

3. _____

My Values Effectiveness

8. _____

4. _____

7. _____

5. _____

6. _____

Kaleidescope Reflections

Once you have chosen up to ten of the values represented on your calendar, evaluate that value on a scale of one to ten on how effective you are in living out that value. Ten is closer to the outside rim, and one is closer to the center of the circle.

Now join the dots of the spokes together. What kind of a circle do you have?

This exercise helps to reveal your effectiveness and also the areas that could use some focused work.

Record your observations and what you intend to do with them. Be sure and celebrate the good and deal with what is off course. Don't waste negative energy on beating yourself up. Take an honest look and take one step forward! This is a great exercise to do on your Window Seat days which we will get to in a bit when we discuss the rhythms of leadership.

Hot Buttons

Hot buttons are those trigger events that hit us directly in our hearts. Many times, the hit that comes at us is not intended personally, and yet the strength of our emotions in the moment can cause our perspective to be blown out of proportion. We take what is said and what is happening directly to heart as a personal attack.

As you move forward to understanding your values and how they affect you, a fun (used loosely!) little exercise which will increase your self-awareness is around recognizing your hot buttons or triggers. As you stop to reflect on what ticks you off, you will most often find that someone or something has stepped on one of your values—something you hold important in life and leadership.

 Kaleidoscope Reflection

1. For a day or two or a week create a trigger log.

2. Pay attention to when you are ticked off, frustrated, impatient.

3. Record what the situation is and how it makes you feel.

4. Now stop to analyze what was the value that you hold dear that was violated for you.

5. Stop to look at the situation, acknowledge your emotions and move to dealing with the facts.

6. Record what you absolutely know for certain.

7. Out of that information, what is one thing you know you need to do?

You will often find this exercise will lead you to seeking out more information that is missing, information that will give you greater understanding in what you can do in order to move forward in a positive manner.

Values Enable Clear Decision Making

IMAGINE . . .

Imagine a world with no decisions.

Monday morning arrives. You're gently woken with a steaming cup of coffee and a breakfast tray. Each item is numbered in the order you should eat it.

You finish eating, and the bed gently lifts you over the edge. When your feet hit the floor, the shower turns on. The soap dish reaches up and hands you the bar of soap and then the shampoo. As you finish, the doors open, and the towel is in your hands.

You walk out to the bedroom, and your clothes are laid out on your bed in the order you are to put them on. You return to the bathroom and your makeup is all lined up in the order and colours you need for today. As you step out of the bathroom, the lights go out.

As you enter the kitchen, your children sit at the table all dressed and waiting for you. As they finish eating, the dishes file off into the dishwasher. Your children get down from the table, and when they get into the bathroom, they pick up their prepared toothbrushes and brush their teeth. As they leave, the bathroom lights go off and they gather their backpacks and coats and get into the car.

Ahh, another wonderful day to live!!!!

Kaleidoscope Reflection

1. What is wrong with the above picture? What makes it so laughable?

2. Take a moment to count how many decisions you made in the first hour you were up today.

3. What were your decisions based on?

4. Describe why that decision you made was important to you.

5. What values did they reflect?

Decision Making Process Based on Our Values

Decision making is often a timely exercise that requires clarity and foresight. Our values can truly guide us in how we make our decisions. Some decisions we make intuitively based on our intrinsic values, others we need a healthy process to assist us. These principles can be put into practice around almost any decision. Often our decisions will have good values and many times those values will be conflicting. When we face conflicting values, it is often difficult because none of them are wrong or evil. The conflict so often is between good and good values.

As I worked with executives in the nonprofit sector, one of my colleagues, Greg, who led a large nonprofit for more than twenty-five years used a simple illustration around the decisions we make. It represents a tension of two values, which will result in very different long-term outcomes.

When faced with a decision the temptation is to take the easy way or the better way.

Easy————————————————————————————————Better

Easy is so tempting because it usually is quick and yet seldom does it yield sustainable, long-term results. Not all decisions face this tension and yet when a decision requires the better choice, the effort it requires yields the most effective outcomes for sustainable, long-term results.

Following this simple process will help to clarify which value is to be upheld in each situation.

Kaleidoscope Reflections

Choose a decision you are facing. Record the details of that decision and then work it through this set of questions.

1. Clarify the decision. What is the actual decision?

2. What are the possible choices that I see?

3. Name the values that govern this decision.

4. Are there conflicting values? Name them.

5. Name the pros around each of these choices? What is the context of those pros from your perspective?

6. What are the cons around each of these choices? What are the cons from your perspective?

7. What resources are needed to carry through on this choice and are they available to me? This may not mean the resources fall in your lap easily. You may have to work at finding the resources and sacrifice for a greater gain.

8. Who are the people I trust and what are the beliefs I hold that influence this choice and how? What do I need to sort through in their opinions?

9. Does my foundation for living (example: Bible) have anything to say about this choice? How do I find this out?

10. What am I choosing and how am I going to move ahead on it?

"The difference between what we do and what we are capable of doing would suffice to solve most of our individual problems."

Mohandas Karamchand Gandhi

Notes—record your most significant thoughts to reflect on and to begin bold action.

Chapter 4

The Journey to Getting Unstuck

Our values are the sweet spot of bringing our perspectives together by focusing on our common values in order to move beyond our differences and work together for the greater good. The heart of unity is found in what we have in common as we serve the greater good. This focus on our common values allows us to get unstuck from the personal hurts, hang-ups and pride that hold us back.

Our common values and perspectives allow our expectations and current reality to work together as we become more self-aware, more aware of others, and more capable of leading in and through our relational strengths and struggles. As we come to new levels of awareness and understanding, we are then required to create healthy communication pathways for protecting the unity we have come to.

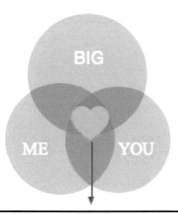

Our **perspectives** when drawn together by our **values** and what we have in common.

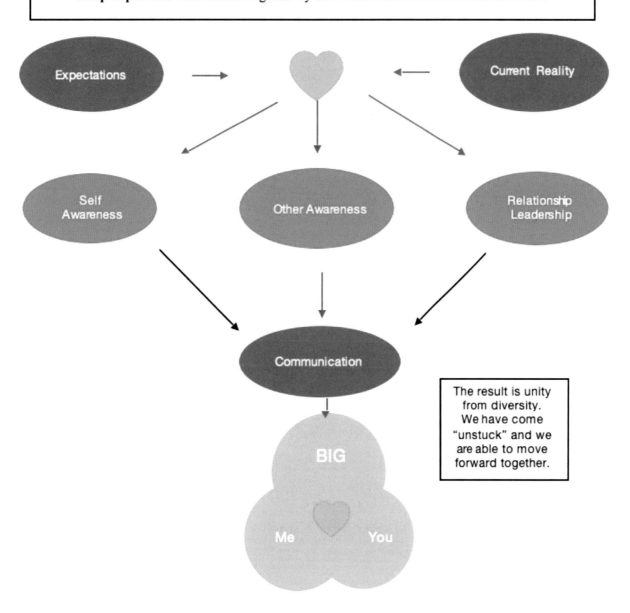

The result is unity from diversity. We have come "unstuck" and we are able to move forward together.

Emotional Intelligence

Kaleidoscope Reflections

1. As you consider the previous template, what areas do you see that you need to spend some time thinking about, defining and developing for greater leadership influence?

2. Create your plan and timeline for this. This is the kind of reflection that is a benefit on a Balcony Day as you observe how and where you need to fit into the bigger picture.

Learning to lead people will always be the most challenging part of any role you fulfill. The three areas above, along with social leadership, will take focused and reflective time in order to lead though the complexity of working with people.

We discussed the area of pride and ego and saw examples of what it looks like in our lives and leadership when we focus on ourselves too much. If the four faces of pride are what derail us, then we need to consider what it looks like when we are leading with healthy confidence. Healthy confidence means we are aware that we, as well as each person we meet, were created with a purpose and a calling. We choose to find the best in each person and be prepared to address less than the best in ourselves and in others as we work together. We use our curiosity to curb our instinct to judge others, which is often based on our perspective alone. Curiosity creates an open invitation for others to be seen and heard and become a part of the solution rather than the problem. We choose to acknowledge our expectations and our current reality in an authentic and realistic way. And so, the conversations go on rather than getting stuck in hurt feelings and unresolved in pain-filled stories.

Understanding and embracing Emotional Intelligence gives us a leadership edge as we learn to acknowledge the feelings that get triggered and stop long enough to uncover the facts and then to weave those together in order to accomplish the ends that are required of us.

As leaders we can usually gain a quick win when we listen to the drama around us and choose to quickly find the fix that makes the problem go away, for the moment. And yet wise is the leader who curiously asks to find out what they don't know in order to create an environment that is strategic and sustainable.

There are a myriad of courses, workshops, 360 Assessments that are worth investing in to develop this area of emotional intelligence (EQ), which will set you apart from merely being a mediocre leader. There is an ever-increasing understanding in the workplace, that without developed emotional intelligence your leadership, your ability to embrace adaptive leadership will be limited. EQ enriches all areas of your life and leadership.

As you focus on the values you have declared are important, on EQ and on communication skills you will find yourself able to keep negotiating into that sweet spot that sets the maximum opportunity for all to move forward.

Notes—record your most significant thoughts to reflect on and to begin bold action.

Chapter 5

Values-Based Communication and Conversations

Challenging or difficult conversations are a regular part of our leadership lives. One question to address is, what is the fine line in determining the right time to have a challenging conversation?

Recognize that all conversations are not equal. Each challenging conversation will have some similarities and also differences. Preparation for a challenging conversation takes a strong self-awareness of what is going on inside yourself, a strong other awareness of your perceptions of what is going on for the others in the conversation, a willingness to hold your need to be right with open hands and curiosity to seek the truth rather than judging from your perspective. This then allows us to bring clarity, respect and thoughtfulness to the conversation while creating an environment to move forward on what we have in common and the ability to lead through our differences.

As we consider how values can enhance and give us the ability to focus on what is important in our conversations, particularly when conflict, hurt, or differences are present, values-based conversations are one of our vehicles to greater clarity and movement forward.

What-if the first values-based conversation was with yourself?

A powerful concept in dealing with any difficult situation is to find clarity in the midst of the circumstances and in the midst of your emotional response. As you already know, when emotions are high, clarity can be enhanced, or it can be lost so quickly. Having the tough conversation with yourself will help you drive to greater clarity and lead to more courageous ways of leading.

 Kaleidoscope Reflection

1. In this situation what are my emotions telling me?

2. What are the facts telling me? Facts are those things that I know to be completely true, with no embellishment.

3. When I put those two together, what do I understand and what information do I need to

search out?

4. What do I need to do to be able to move forward with integrity, humility, grace and truth? You also could ask, what do I need to do to move forward and list what you value most.

Bold—The Courageous Risk to Face Reality

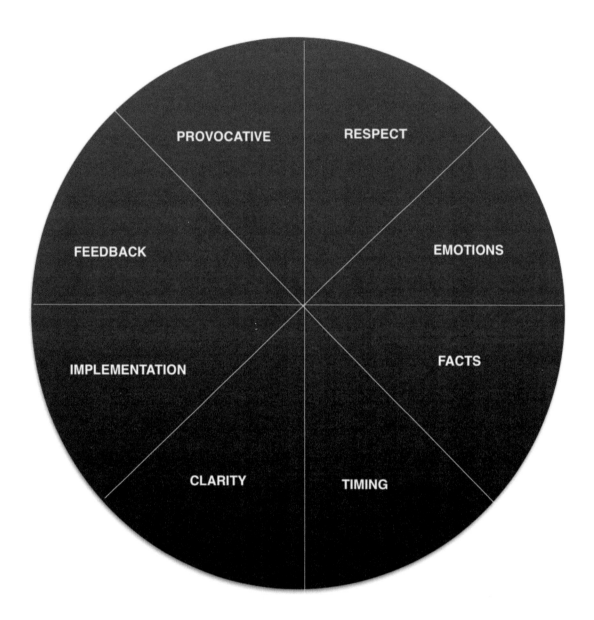

Bold action comes from bold internal and external conversations and reflections. There are certain principles that can enable you to find freedom in moving forward.

1. Respect

In any situation be clear on what it means to act with respect, even if your respect for the other person(s) in the situation has been broken. Choosing the higher road in our conversations and behaviours reaps the reward of knowing you have done it well and an inner peace is the result and a reduction of stress. When we enter a difficult conversation, we need to be mindful that when trust has been broken, when emotions are high, we will tend to embellish the story, to move away from the facts, and our respect for the others can diminish dramatically.

On a scale of 1–10 how would you rate your respect in the following areas?

- for yourself
- for the other person(s)
- for the situation

Think about some ways you can move to respect when you have been hurt or disappointed in yourself, in others, or in the situation.

2. Emotion

Our first response to any situation is a sense that comes through our sense of sight, touch, taste, sound or smell. This is raw data. To illustrate, look at a portion from the article *Mental Health, A New Understanding* as found in Time magazine.

Time Magazine; Mental Health, A New Understanding

> *Lisa Barrett, professor of psychology from Northeastern University, explains: "At times we know exactly how we feel: we are angered by blocked goals, saddened by a loss or unafraid of an impending challenge. And that is good because when we can describe our feelings with precision, it gives us information we can act on. At other times, however, our feelings are a hopeless muddle. In these cases, we seem only able to describe our feelings as, just bad. It becomes hard, then, to use those feelings to work out what to do next. The ability to make fine distinctions among emotions—enables your brain, as Barrett puts it. "to construct the most useful instance of the most useful emotion concept" —is exceedingly fluid. It can vary by circumstances for any given individual, and it can vary among individuals. This is a skill that children typically learn during normal development, but it is also a skill that adults can learn to hone. And guess how we do that? "Perhaps the easiest way," Barrett writes, "is to learn new words. Words seed your concepts, concepts drive your predictions, predictions regulate your body budget (which is how your brain anticipates and fulfills your body's energy needs), and your body budget determines how you feel."*

On a Scale of 1¬–10 how would you describe your feelings or emotions?

The strength of your emotion is in this situation. What are the stories you are telling yourself and/or others that feed the waves of emotion? Name the emotions you are experiencing.

3. Facts

The facts are what is exactly true. Learn to repeat each rendering of the situation to ask yourself, "What do I know to be exactly true?" Doing fact checks allows you to see that your emotions have not clouded your thinking, or in other words you are checking out the stories your emotions are telling. Be in tune with how you experience stress. The higher the stress the easier it is to embellish the truth or to make up stories.

Fact Checking

Describe the situation. Once you have described it, go through and highlight the facts only.

On a scale of 1–10 how factual are you being about the situation? What information are you missing? What do you know for sure that will guide your next step or decision?

4. Timing

"Ready, aim, fire" would be a healthy sequence of events when you have had a hot button hit or one of your values has been stepped on. This is not our natural reaction to a trigger event; our natural reaction is flight or fight. In developing greater self-awareness, we can learn to use time as our ally to the resolution of challenging circumstances.

A principle that has served me well as I have chosen to use it is: Buy Time. Rather than respond out of high emotion, learn a few phrases that can bring the temperature of the situation down and remind you of what is most important.

Phrases like:
- Hmmm, that is a different way of thinking for me. Let me give it some thought.
- Thank you for giving me that information. Let me give it some thought.
- Thank you for sharing your thoughts on this. I had not thought of it that way and need to take some time to consider what you said.

You get the idea? Allow yourself not to have to buy into the urgency of emotion. There will be times that demand an immediate response and yet they are truly rare. Do be prepared for them as well. A caution: if you have asked for time to think about a situation, then do that; do not neglect to get back to the other person(s) in a timely manner. This approach is not about trying to get out of a circumstance you do not want to face. Lead with integrity as you learn new ways to handle difficult situations.

High emotion can be fuel to the timing.

On a scale of 1–10 what would you say the urgency of this situation is?

What emotions are making this situation more urgent than it truly is?

What is your phrase for buying time to respond with more clarity?

5. Clarity

We are familiar with how muddy and how often we can get confused in our thinking when our emotions are high. Once you have bought yourself some time, drive to clarity.

Drive to Clarity

Take time to identify your emotion(s).

On a scale of 1–10 how clear are you on the one thing you can do?

What is the one next thing you can do?

6. Implementation

Being bold is a thought-filled process that eventually becomes a part of your healthy response ability. Having spent the time to think through being bold to this point means that to carry through there must be a plan, which creates a healthy accountability.

Your plan can include your response to the situation now that you have had time to think it through:

> What will you say?
>
> Why is that important?
>
> Who needs to be in the conversation?
>
> How will you extend an invitation to this conversation?
>
> When will you say it?
>
> Where will you meet?
>
> What information will you ask for that you realize you do not have?
>
> What will be the next step?

Create your plan.

Based on a scale of 1–10 how solid is your plan?

Describe your plan.

Where does it fit on the calendar?

7. Feedback

Having solid accountability people and processes in your life becomes more and more significant as your leadership influence increases. Feedback is very different from gossip and casually telling the situation thereby getting reactive advice. This is not water cooler chat.

Feedback is the authentic recounting to trusted advisors (coach, mentor) for insight into what they see clouding your vision and/or what information you are missing to make a solid next step forward.

 Kaleidoscope Reflections

1. On a scale of 1–10 how effective is your use of feedback?

2. Who are your trusted advisors?

3. Who have you asked, or who will you ask, to speak into your life and this situation?

4. Where is this on your calendar?

8. Provocative

As you take this step back and consider the whole situation, what is it provoking in you as an influential leader?

On a scale of 1–10, what is your level of provocation?

Use your kaleidoscope thinking to shift the original picture to a stepping-stone for you to see more fully, to grow and be more effective, and to do more intentionally and productively.

Describe how this situation and/or person(s) are provoking you to see, be and do differently. What have you learned?

What do you want to embrace more fully?

What-if your conversation was on how you could accomplish your common purpose together for the good of the client you serve?

I have worked in organizations where at times the tasks have held a higher value than the people engaged in those tasks. This often resulted in people being treated as objects rather than humans. Because of my value of relationship, this often troubled me and created stressful situations and conversations. My relational value did not mean the work should be less than it could be, it meant that I would have conversations with those involved to see how we could address situations in order to move forward together. As I sought to honour the organizational values, my values and the other person's values, we could have conversations that did not forget the humanity of all in the light of the tasks that needed to be completed.

Values-based conversations allow us to take a step back, to consider what we perceive, what we know, what we value and to hear what others in the situation perceive, know and value. Our challenge then is to do the dance of give and take to bring those values, demands, perceptions and knowledge to a place of collaboration.

The diagram that follows provides a practical template to consider as you seek to have values-based conversations.

BIG circle stands for the mission, vision, values that represent and guide the work and/or the relationship.

ME circle stands for you the leader in the situation and what you perceive and what you value.

YOU circle stands for the other person(s) and what they perceive and what they value.

The *green shape* in the middle stands for a sweet spot. The sweet spot is that place where you draw together in collaboration in order to handle the present situation and create a space to move forward together for the sake of what you say you value together. This gives the opportunity to focus on what draws you together and to manage what divides you.

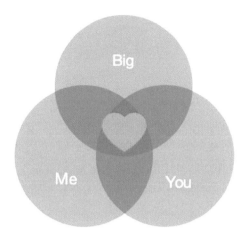

Rarely is this a one-time conversation. It is an ongoing conversation even once you have reached a sweet spot to continue the dance of give and take in a respectful and life-giving way, considering all perspectives and together deciding which direction you will choose and how you will get there.

Early on in leadership I realized a way to have healthy conversations that were far more about collaboration as opposed to who was right. I also discovered about myself that I am not an arguer or a fighter and yet I am a scrapper. The point in scrapping for me is what I can learn that I do not already know. It has allowed me the freedom to present my perspective, listen to another, and put my figuring out thoughts on the table! As others presented their perspective, I then had other information to weigh my perspective with and to come out with a broader perspective. Although this scrapping worked on some levels as I moved in leadership circles, scrapping did not always prove the most productive way to converse with others and find ways forward through an issue. When I was introduced to this three-circle model, it resonated with who I was, and yet when I got off track, it was simple enough to remind me of what I must pursue to have a free heart and be able to move forward working with and through others.

Our values have the potential to create conflict as we work with others, and they also have the potential to create great collaboration.

I have had the joy of working with executives in the nonprofit world. This has provided a number of relationships that see eye to eye with me on many things and also relationships that had very differing worldviews.

One day as we were at the beginning of a new executive cohort, we were discussing the commitments and values we would honour in the next eighteen months we would be spending together. As we came to the end of discussing the commitments and values, a young man who was new to the executive director role asked, "What do you think of swearing? Can we swear at this table?" Personally, I do not value swearing as a form of communication. I consider it the lazy way of communicating negative emotions that could be used for positive energy rather than negative reactions. As lead facilitator I had the responsibility to hold the values of the organization up and be true to myself and yet not impose my way as being the right way in all things because it is only one way. There was an inner pause as I considered the question. Very quickly this model popped into my head. I knew what the organization stood for in professionalism. I knew what I stood for in the use of language. I was not aware of what the young man stood for as I had only recently met him.

The response that came to mind actually represented a truth I had learned the hard way as a young leader. "If you want to be heard, be sure that when you speak you pay attention to whether anyone is listening to you!" And so my response was in this vein, "I encourage you to speak and when you do, if you want to be heard then pay attention to how people respond to the way you communicate, your language and your tone." This was not the answer the young man or the room was prepared for. I so loved it because it did not carry any weight of judgment, it simply put ownership back where it belonged. At a leadership table the attitudes and behaviours will reveal levels of maturity and credibility. Each leader is responsible for the perceptions they leave with others. That is a key work of leadership being aware and taking responsibility for the perceptions that are left behind. It is the wake of our leadership that either increases our leadership influence or gets us stuck in a lesser place of influence.

This model has also allowed a way to seek out other perspectives before there is a difficult situation, creating a space to let go of my need to be right and honour a higher value that leads to crafting and shaping a meaningful conversation. As we consider values-based conversations, the following exercise places you as the initiator or the lead in addressing the situation and working with those involved.

There is no set formula that works in every situation and yet there are principles that we can follow to reach a collaborative outcome that moves each person and the organization or situation forward.

Principles of Preparation for a Values-Based Conversation

1. **Reaffirmation:** As you consider the top circle of the circle of three, review and reaffirm what the BIG is and what it stands for—values, mission and vision.

2. **Description:** Circle two: Describe the situation from your perspective, what you see, what you experience, how it makes you feel—it is okay to be raw here.

3. **Feelings**: Consider your emotions around this situation. Describe what and how you are feeling. Acknowledge the power any one of those emotions is having for the good, or not for the good.

4. **Facts**: Now go back through your description, sentence by sentence, or bullet by bullet. Ask yourself, "What is the absolute truth in this statement?" Or "What do I know to be completely true?" "What interpretation has my emotion added on?" Highlight the facts in one colour; highlight the emotions in another colour.

5. **Discovery:** What did you discover in this exercise?

Generally, people discover that their emotions on their own are only a part of the story—a significant part and yet a part, not the whole. As you pursue acknowledging your emotions and uncovering the facts, you come to a space of realizing you do not have all the information you need. Your emotions imagined some things that may or may not have been true. When this happens:

Step 1 Go to the appropriate person to get the information that is needed. See below for crafting the conversation to fulfill circle three.

Step 2 In light of this new information, determine the one thing you can do in order to help move this situation in a positive direction.

Step 3 Do that one thing that moves the situation and the relationship forward.

Principles for a Values-Based Conversation

1. **Prepare:** See Principles of Preparation for a Values-Based Conversation.

2. **Choose:** Who the conversation needs to be with and an appropriate time when you are both able to focus and move through the needed information.

3. **Start:** To begin the face-to-face (preferable when it is a difficult conversation), be prepared to acknowledge with appreciation the other person's time and availability. This is a healthy way of reminding yourself that you are equally created with the same concerns, needs and desires—a reminder that you are both human! No objectifying.

4. **Review:** As you are the one to instigate the conversation, present a one-minute brief of the intent and desired outcome of this conversation.

5. **Present**: Present the situation acknowledging that this is your present perspective.

6. **Invite:** Invite the other person to present their perspective while you listen intently and stop yourself from preparing to talk.

Preparing to talk means that you are only listening with the intent to defend your perspective. It hinders you from truly hearing where the other person is coming from. Pay attention to words, intonation, body language, response to environment, eye contact.

7. **Curious:** Be curious in your response rather than judgmental. It is so easy when you hear something that pokes at your emotional trigger to begin to judge not only what the other person says, but also who they are. Judgmental comments will STOP any form of movement forward.

Curiosity means asking with childlike wonder.
Questions of wonderment.
Let go of preconceived thoughts or judgments.
Simply I wonder, name what you wonder.

8. **Acknowledge:** Acknowledge their perspective without commentary and invite them into a review of the perspective and values of circle one, your perspective and values, their perspective and values. Invite them into a collaborative dialogue of how to bring those perspectives together in order to have positive movement forward.

9. **Act:** Create an action plan.

10. **Accountability:** Affirm the timeline of action items and when you will check in with each other next.

As I was writing this portion of this book, I was sent an email with unexpected information that would profoundly affect me, my colleagues, and my clients. I came back and read this chapter and reminded myself, "This is what I am telling others; how is it working for me right now?" It does work and it is working. There are a number of stopping places in the process that mean I have to do some work and I have to make some decisions on what my reactions, actions, and/or responses would be. Being values focused in how I serve my clients has moved me beyond getting stuck so many times. I realized that because over time I have addressed my issues and worked to find a healthy process that serve all perspectives represented, this was initially upsetting. Then I simply slipped into walking the processes I shared above to a "guilt free, take the high road, expect the best, and be prepared for the best outcomes" approach. Growing in awareness of ourselves, of others in our sphere of influence, and how to lead through relationships and situations is an ongoing, formative experience for every leader. Becoming is the journey we are on as leaders. Our roles change, our organizations change, our people change. Change is the constant we move and breathe in. As leaders we cannot remain stagnant or think we have arrived. Finding a way to remain relevant, fresh, adaptive is a constant.

In the following section on Integration, you will find a way to become all you need to be in each season, in each change. Here is your invitation to a deep leadership dive.

Notes—record your most significant thoughts to reflect on and to begin bold action.

_____

_____

_____

_____

_____

_____

_____

_____

_____

_____

_____

_____

_____

_____

_____

_____

_____

_____

_____

_____

Section 2—*INTEGRATION*

Contents

Chapter 6
Introduction to Integration

Integration is the practical process of turning inspiration into transformation. It is common to be inspired by beauty, by simplicity, by craftsmanship, by eloquence in speech and word, by ideas, and by so much more. Inspiration on its own fades and leaves a gap or a tension point between what was so uplifting and yet has not resulted in action. Integration provides a pathway to continue to move forward and to grapple with the realities of life and leadership, which do not always turn out the way we envisioned.

The Self-Leadership Growth Path is a part of the **What-if** Leadership Series. It represents the integration of all we are and all we desire to be as leaders. It is thought-provoking and hard work. Your first time through will create a baseline for you to use as you live out the Infinity Leadership Development Loop found at the end of Section 1 on Inspiration.

What-if it was possible to stay fresh and dynamic in your leadership journey?

As an emerging leader, a mid-level leader, an executive leader, a seasoned leader, growth is our byword. Once we choose to stop growing, we stop leading. Our times, our culture, our work environments and we as leaders, are constantly changing whether we choose to pay attention or not. A choice to not grow is a choice to stagnate and lose touch with reality.

So much of our time and energy is spent on completing the daily work that piles up on our desks and in our minds. We find our time and energy diminished for lack of attention, reflection and clear strategic intention and direction. Our lives become wrapped in what lies directly in front of us. We can so easily lose touch with generative thinking, with lifting our minds and hearts to ongoing possibilities and opportunities.

The Self-Leadership Growth Path, is found at the end of this Introduction. The Self-Leadership Growth Path is about taking the time out to see our leadership role, our leadership qualities, and our leadership environments. It is about increasingly becoming more intentionally focused as we become more competent and confident in how we exercise the leadership that has been entrusted to us.

We begin with the Self-Leadership Growth Path. It gives an overview of the strategic approach we will take to grow in our leadership. This strategic way of thinking is the same methodology we use when we make strategic plans for our organizations and even simple decisions we make every day. It often is intuitive. In this section we are applying the strategy to ourselves and our growth as leaders.

Each section is broken down with thought-provoking questions for you to reflect upon. This process will lead you to create or re-create a personal leadership mission or purpose statement that will act as a compass for the leadership role you are called to fulfill. The material is best used as you take time to reflect and consider your perceptions of yourself as a leader and of how others perceive your leadership. Next it will be helpful to discuss your reflections with another leader to encourage each other as you increase in your confidence and competence. You will find this is an invaluable aid in creating an accountability framework as you continue to grow and develop as a leader.

Recently in a leadership cohort I facilitate in the nonprofit sector, I had asked the second level leaders to come prepared to share their leadership statements. They had prepared them as they worked through the Self-leadership Pathway. This was a day to celebrate all the work they had completed in the last six months. After each one shared the statement they had written to guide them in their leadership, they broke into pairs to talk about how they would keep these statements alive. The goal was not to let them become a nice thought tucked away in a pile of papers or on their phones. It was so gratifying and inspiring to hear the various ways they were choosing to allow these reflective statements to continue to guide them. Each one chose a way that was unique to who they were and how they could focus the best on what they had said was important to them. For example: a sticky note on their mirror; a copy hung on the wall behind where they hang their jacket at the beginning and end of every day—a great check in and reminder; a plan to talk about it with others to embed it in their mind; revisit it every morning and evening for thirty days so it becomes a part of their thinking; use it as a measuring stick as they plan the future. There were so many great ideas to let these well thought out statements transform their leadership and keep them moving forward.

Over the years I have intuitively focused, shaped, pursued the 'what next' that lay before me. As I came to the place of turning my unnamed process into a tool to be handed on to others, great clarity and energy emerged. The questions were originally created for myself as I sought clarity about opportunities and decisions that I was facing in a changing season of life and leadership.

From taking the time to intentionally focus, reflect, and take bold action, I discovered I had found clarity to guide my next season. A tag line emerged that became a measuring stick of accountability for me.

Intentionally inspiring leaders to focus, to reflect and to take bold action.

This statement, along with my values, enabled me to make clear decisions around what I was to take on and what I was to let go of or pass by. I also discovered I now had a tool that would aid others in their leadership journeys.

In 2016 I had the privilege of being the lead facilitator for a second level cohort of executive leaders. As my partner and I sat to plan and think through what this six-month cohort could do for these leaders, we realized that a focused growth plan would give them a framework to invest in themselves and their ongoing development. Each month we would focus on one of the quadrants found in the aforementioned template. The participants were given a workbook with significant questions for each quadrant. Then they were asked to partner with another participant in the cohort to discuss their self-learnings from those particular questions. At the next cohort we would call them back to share with the large cohort what they had observed, thought about and discovered. We encouraged them to talk about the places where their thinking had shifted, or about the choices they were making that would help them increase in their leadership effectiveness. The results were so incredible as they focused, took time to reflect and then found clarity for places of bold action that were intentional and transformative. We saw the power of reflection around their leadership, partnered with relationship, was a powerful tool for creating a baseline to continue to build on. This truly had become a tool to encourage others to be strategic in their thinking and leadership and not to have to continually run to others for problems to be solved.

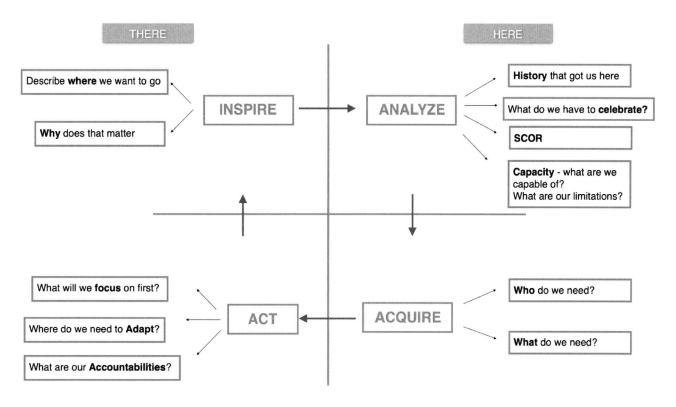

Notes—record your most significant thoughts to reflect on and to begin bold action.

Chapter 7

Self-Leadership Growth Path Overview

What-if I become an inspiring leader who is in touch with my part to a bigger purpose in our world?

To be inspired is about being filled and given life by something bigger than ourselves. We find great fulfillment as we have something of worth and purpose to pour out on others. In the quadrant **Inspire** you will look at who you desire to be in this season of your leadership journey and also consider *why that matters*. A key component of this quadrant will be what belief system you have as a foundation to build on. This will reveal what you value most and how as you live those values you become more integrated. Your values give understanding to why that matters.

Inspiration, visions and dreams are all starting points to experiencing fulfillment. Paying attention to these and following through in a strategic way will give discernment and clarity for what could be. It is the ready-aim-fire approach we talked about when we looked at values in Section 1.

It seems that over and over again, I have had the opportunity of interacting, building relationships and influencing women by simply paying attention to my thoughts and dreams. In 1996 a question was asked in a casual conversation. I came to realize I was being offered a dream I had not spoken out loud until that point. Would I want to take on the leadership of programming for women as a volunteer? I didn't hear the programming part. I heard the opportunity and privilege to be involved with women that would allow me to walk with them, influence them, see them grow and become all they were created to be. That was only the beginning of a significant, challenging and fulfilling leadership journey. It did not come as a bolt out of the blue, it just came in a very casual conversation and yet I recognized it was for me.

In the quadrant **Analyze** you will take a detailed look at your leadership lifeline as a part of your history. You will explore:

- your life events
- what you have to celebrate
- what brought sadness into your life
- the situations in your life that caused you to grow the leadership roles you fulfilled

All these will launch you on a journey of seeing all you have become and how that will open up the future for you. You will complete *SCOR*. A look at your:

Strengths and abilities as well as your Challenges, which speak to what is intrinsic to you. Your Opportunities and your Roadblocks which speak to your extrinsic influences.

Capacity is a significant and often overlooked concept in fulfilling vision. You will consider what part of your capacity is static and what is adaptive.

Analyze is the space that is challenging and takes great patience and perseverance. It is the nitty-gritty of the details. This is the space to seek greater input on the way you are wired and what you are passionate about. It is also the place where you have the privilege of learning to work with others who have strengths and abilities you do not have. I discovered that as I began to gather this information about myself it gave me a realistic and confident picture of who I was and what I could do. It also provided the caution that I was not created to do things alone. I learned there is greater accomplishment and fulfillment in learning to work in relationship with others.

In the quadrant **Acquire** you will look at who you need working alongside you and what you need to accomplish your vision for who you want to be in this leadership season. This is the quadrant that leads you to those with whom you can create a team.

All my life I have had this uncanny intuition that has happened quite regularly. I will meet someone for the first time, have a great conversation and learn more about them. Our paths may not cross for a long time. Sometime later as I am contemplating something I am starting out on, I realize I need a certain kind of person to be on the team. I will experience a thought and the face of someone I have met. I will make a phone call to them, have a conversation with them and know they are to be on the team. And then to find that this was exactly what they were looking for was icing on the cake and confirmation that this was the right direction.

As a young leader I was asked to chair a committee that was part of a national organization. As I was putting that committee together and needed a vice chair, a women I had met at a conference in the previous year came to mind. We had been introduced and very quickly had found out where our hearts had resonated together in leadership and in working with women. I had not thought a lot about that conversation until I began thinking about who might make a great vice chair. It only took a phone call to her, and in a conversation that left us both energized I had a wonderful vice chair. We served together for a number of fulfilling years.

In the quadrant **Act** you will take time to consider where your *focus* will be, where you will need to practice *adaptability* and what *accountability* you will put in place to achieve your strategic intentions. **Act** is where the rubber meets the road. It is where we finally get to take bold action. After all that hard brain work of **Analyze** is completed, now it is the time to FIRE.

Over the years I have worked with a wide variety of personalities and people with various ways of approaching leadership. Some have been dreamers who have not known how to get from the dream to the bold action. Some have been the analyzers who get stuck in the weeds. Some have been the Fire… Fire…Fire people who leave devastation in their wake. All have had incredible gifts and when brought together in a team, they have accomplished great things.

Our leadership is dynamic and influenced by the roles we play, the context and organization we serve in, our longevity in either the organization or our role. To remain credible and true to what you say is important. You will find that times of reflection make you a better leader.

There are hundreds of books that hold the name leader or leadership development in them and yet there is still a struggle to find solid leadership. The Self-Leadership Growth Path is a way to give you strategic thinking tools to move forward in your development as a leader. It will enable you to think about those universal principles that will keep your leadership fresh and dynamic.

Once you have completed this exercise you can use it as a baseline for ongoing growth and development as a leader. You will become more intentional about maximizing how you spend your time and money in professional development. This becomes a focused approach rather than a wide-angle buckshot approach. This tool can also be used to help your employees and volunteers to be strategic in their approach to problem solving and clarity to step into greater ownership and responsibility. In the following chapters we will work our way through the Self-Leadership Pathway. Be prepared to set the time and energy aside to dive in and to work your heart and brain towards greater integration.

"To be wise is to be eternally curious."
American Theologian and Writer, Frederick Buechner

Notes—record your most significant thoughts to reflect on and to begin bold action.

Chapter 8
Quadrant 1, INSPIRE . . . THERE

What-if I was clear on my THERE and pursued it with intentionality and focus?

Inspire is about the ability to envision who you are to be as a leader and what you are to do. It equates with a vision for yourself as a leader and why that matters. Inspire is about being a part of something that is bigger than yourself. It is knowing your call and your passion. As we consider being inspired, it is about discovering who we were created to be, what is unique to us and how our life experience has crafted and shaped us. This is a place to understand what spirituality looks like in your life right now and how it is influencing your future. You may have already discovered a longing inside to know yourself, what makes you tick and where you fit in this world. This may be a time of reaffirming who you are and where you are heading. This may be a seasonal time of change in your life and focus.

Looking at life and who we long to be is influenced by so much. In hindsight, our inner fears are often great clarifiers. There are times when fear is experienced as a warning to back away, to protect ourselves. Fear is also a way of getting a laser focus on how you can be a significant part of something so much bigger and more powerful than yourself. Fears may be based on our past experiences that have not been processed. Or they may be based on finding freshly discovered values or beliefs rising up inside that give us direction.

The first step is learning to pay attention to who you long to be in this season of your leadership. This enables a realization of how "gradually, then suddenly" what we might have thought of as a crazy idea, begins to show up in so many different ways and places in our lives. Going back to my journey of Inspired to Lead, it began by one multi-coloured word on a white flyleaf of a book that caught my attention. I love colour. I love creativity. I love things that stop me in my tracks and make me take a second look. And so, I bought a book that sat on my desk for three months before randomly being thrown in a box of books just in case I might pick it up while on vacation. Little did I know it would be the jump start, a catalyst, a forerunner of a new season of my life. It would become my standard for how I would lead and invest in others. "Gradually, then suddenly" our lives unfold as we pay attention to the little, the quirky, to whatever catches our attention and stops us in our tracks.

I was learning to:

STOP–REFLECT–RECALCULATE

I invite you to begin this intentional journey of paying attention to what may already have been on your peripheral vision, to what might be right in front of you, to what you may have considered too small because you had a scarcity mindset. Join me in digging a little deeper inside to discover nuances and outright spaces of brilliance that have the potential to enrich and transform your life and leadership.

What follows is a number of thought-provoking exercises that will help you reflect on your personal leadership story and envision what it could look like in the future. As you work through these exercises, your leadership growth will become clearer and more compelling. You will become more competent and confident and will increase in your capacity to lead.

 Kaleidoscope Reflections

These questions are a baseline to put down what may be stirring in your head and heart. They will be followed by greater clarifying exercises throughout this section.

1. What words would you use to describe this season of your life or of your leadership journey? A fun little optional exercise is to take these words and create a Wordle as a reminder to you of what you said about yourself.

2. Describe what is happening in your life and world at this time. Don't just look for the negative, look for the beauty of life that surrounds you as well.

3. Describe the THERE you see in this present leadership role you hold or a role you would aspire to.

4. Describe who you want to be in this present leadership season of your life. Just provide loose thoughts and notes. There is no need for polish and wordsmithing at this stage.

5. Brainstorm the way you wish to be recognized, to be perceived by others in your leadership role. Focus on your character, abilities, skills, and opportunities.

   a. Describe the character qualities that are important to you as a leader.

   b. Describe your innate abilities. What comes most natural or easy for you and has the greatest potential for maximum development?

   c. What skills have you acquired and what skills do you excel in?

   d. What opportunities have you seen that attract you or have been offered to you?

3. Consider the role description of what you want to be prepared for. Where do you see alignment with who you are and where do you identify gaps? Name them. Who do you know that could work and collaborate alongside you to fill the gaps?

4. Reflect on what you have discovered and answer the question, "Why does this matter?" For each

observation go back to the values exercises you did in Section 1 and list those values here.

5. Begin crafting a first draft describing who you want to be in this season of your leadership.

As I pursued answering these questions for myself, I found a fresh clarity and ability to see how so much of my life had been preparing me for this season. I began to discover purpose and meaning to what previously had seemed like disconnected events. Comments that people had made to me over time, that I had not understood in the moment, were now making sense to me.

Over time as a young leader of the committee I had previously mentioned, I had the privilege of meeting many strong, capable women leaders who were farther down the road than I was in my leadership. It was my responsibility to see that everything was lined up for them to be successful, for them to speak and inspire women in their everyday lives, careers and volunteer roles. As I met them for the first time and spoke with them, invariably they would ask if they could speak into my life and then they would speak words of affirmation, encouragement and blessing. I often went home and told my husband about those conversations and I would say, "I don't get it." "It" being what they had said about and to me. As I pursued the Self-Leadership Pathway, many of those comments came back to me and I had many aha moments as they began to fit together with greater areas of self-discovery that I was making.

Notes—record your most significant thoughts to reflect on and to begin bold action.

_____

_____

_____

_____

_____

_____

_____

_____

_____

_____

_____

_____

_____

_____

_____

_____

_____

_____

_____

_____

Chapter 9
Quadrant 2, ANALYZE . . . HERE

What-if I was to take the time to appreciate the gift of life I have been given and the calling to leadership that rests on my shoulders like a mantle?

Adapting Webster's definition of the word *analyze* we see it as "to study (something) closely and carefully: to learn the nature and relationship of the parts of (something) by a close and careful examination: to study the emotions and thoughts of (someone) by using psychoanalysis."

Analyze is how you come to see the integration of all that has brought you to this point, all that you have to celebrate and all that you are moving into the future with. Be aware that this is the hard, often tedious space of the Self- Leadership Pathway. Stick with me; it brings rich results. Generally speaking, many who would call themselves visionaries have a challenging time here dwelling in what feels like the weeds. Their vision and passion wants to leap forward without laying this solid foundation.

Analyze covers four areas for you to reflect on.

1. History

2. Celebration

3. Current Reality—*SCOR* (*S*trengths, *C*hallenges, *O*pportunities, and *R*oadblocks)

4. Capacity—Static and Adaptive

1. History

The Leadership Lifeline Exercise found on the next page, will be a guide for you as you look at your history. This is not something you can complete in one sitting. It takes mindful remembering, reflecting and recording. As you look back over your life you will discover a fresh appreciation and understanding of who you are today and also of some of the dreams and hopes you have for the future.

 Kaleidoscope Reflections

Leadership Lifeline Materials

- A large 12" x 24" piece of card stock

- Small sticky notes: yellow, pink, blue, green, purple, or mauve.

Leadership Lifeline Process

- To begin just start writing down one memory at a time as they come to you on the yellow stickies. If you know the approximate date or year, record that as well. Place these on the card stock. For example: 5th birthday party—new parka, first coat that wasn't a hand-me-down; family camping at Kootenay Lake; fostering a newborn for a couple of weeks; camp days with Mr. Anderson; my cousin Grant killed in a car accident (I was nine); my Auntie Jean killed by a drunk driver (I was twenty-seven); competing as a five-year-old at the Royal Conservatory Music Festival; voted in as president of our youth group; watching the kids on the riverbank behind our church, who had so little and nothing to play with; in bed with rheumatic fever for a year.

- As you go through the yellow stickies place a pink sticky by any memory that made you happy or fulfilled, these are the moments to celebrate. Add any additional information For example: family camping on Kootenay Lake—swimming in the rain, campfires, the warmth of family.

- Go through the yellow stickies again and place blue stickies by any of the memories that held sadness, grief, or disappointments. For example: Both the death of my cousin Grant when I was nine and my Auntie Jean when I was twenty-seven created a fear of car accidents that I never realized I carried with me and only learned to deal with many years later.

- Now take your green stickies and place them where you recognize there was growth in you in one way or another. For example: Having this precious little newborn to foster for two weeks when I was 14 brought a sense of nurturing and delight into my heart that was new (that was a pink sticky). It also brought a sense of a depth of grief I had not been familiar with when she left (a blue sticky) and the beginning learnings of what a mix of joys and sorrows our lives hold. Somehow, we survive and even thrive, if we can learn to figure it out (green sticky). Take your purple stickies and place them beside any memories that called you to be a leader. For example: Watching those kids on the riverbank led me to talk to my mom and another woman I admired about what I saw and was feeling and what I wanted to do—I wanted to start a club for them. This led me to coming to Calgary with my mom to take leadership training as a fifteen-year-old. The organization I took the training from was puzzled and excited that a fifteen-year-old would want to do this, and yet they had an age rule, which said I had to be twenty one. They had to figure that one out. I am so grateful that they saw the exception to the rule and so I began my leadership journey.

- Now take these groupings of stickies and arrange them in a chronological order and look for natural breaks. For example: I first ordered my stickies into decades and then I gave each section a name. I recognized that the theme of *heart* came up time and again. A new heart, a damaged heart, a passionate heart, a broken heart, a fulfilled heart, etc. I have seen others write their story by using music themes or book title themes.

- What are you learning about yourself and your leadership history in this exercise? Start writing your story.

As I traced the journey of my heart, I could see a theme in the life I had been given and the journey I was on. In hindsight, I could see how purpose was being crafted for me all along, even if I didn't understand it. I recognized that many of the most powerful lessons in my life came from the disappointments, hurts and the life happenings I really wish had never happened. I saw how my life had had purpose and plan all along and part of my journey was the privilege to take the time to reflect and figure out what was mine to know and pursue.

2. World History

1. Research the year you were born and briefly describe the world you were born into and reflect on how that has shaped and molded you.

For example: I was born very soon after World War II ended. My upbringing reflected a frugality of waste not, want not. This influenced the way I approached financial management as an adult.

Disposables were costly in my world. Permanent containers meant less expenditure. Hand-me-down furniture was acceptable, new furniture and a fully design conscious house brought up conversations on where this money could be used more effectively. Over time it has been fascinating to watch the measurement of cost shift. As women in North America began to move into the workforce, they carried many responsibilities inside and outside the home. Time as a resource took on a new meaning. Disposables were now time savers and practical help. Today our environment is a resource that has risen in value and so disposables are no longer acceptable as they diminish our environment. We continue to shift in our understanding, and we have the option to choose what we value most. These shifts in our world change the way we live and allow us to be aware and intentional of the choices we make.

2. How would you describe how your time in history has provided the foundation you are building your life and leadership upon? What are you being enabled to do and what are you being challenged to do by this foundation?

3. When you look back over your life, what leadership roles did you hold? Refer to the purple stickies in the Leadership Lifeline Exercise.

4. What did you learn in those roles that influence how you look at the future? What did you learn not to do by what you observed or experienced versus what you learned to do?

5. How would you describe those learnings for the future you are considering? Which were character traits of those you observed, and which were situational circumstances?

3. Celebrations

These are the pink stickies in the Leadership Lifeline Exercise. Celebration has numerous functions in our leadership journey.

- Gratitude—As we look back, we deepen our leadership mindset when we recognize all that we have to be grateful for. Hindsight often opens up a whole new world of gratitude. We begin to recognize how even the most challenging situations give us the opportunity to rise to new levels of self-awareness, other-awareness and to choose who we will allow this to make us. For example: It is similar to the shift of the kaleidoscope as we learn to move through each circumstance no matter how rich and fulfilling, or painful and challenging. Gratitude allows us to get to the space where we can see and become grateful for even the smallest gift. I remember when the word arrived that my auntie had been killed by a drunk driver and my warm, gentle, and strong Dad had to go and identify his sister. I felt anger, grief and a wish to pay back. And yet I discovered pools of gratefulness within as I realized the strength and compassionate wonder within my Dad. It was his grace and example of practical love, his ability to deal with his emotion and walk through the pain to a place of forgiveness that caused me to think differently. What a gift it was to me to experience his outlook and way of being.

- The ability to move forward—When we look back and celebrate all that has been, we allow ourselves and others to release the past. Celebration helps us recognize what we have done and recognize it is a great foundation to build on. This time has been significant and retains its significance as a foundation to move forward into the next season. Over time as I watched this journey of the reality of unnecessary death and deep emotional pain in my Dad, I also saw that as he acknowledged it, he also discovered the will and ability to forgive. This freed him to move beyond being stuck in a place of pain and blame and bitterness. He had a strong faith that even in the toughest of times brought a measure of hope and deep joy.

- Relational Wisdom—As we look back and celebrate, we have a greater understanding of who has played significant roles in our leadership and in our personal lives. We learn how to navigate the relational minefields in more effective and life-giving ways. We discover the freedom of acknowledging our hurts, hang-ups, and judgmental opinions. We begin to see them in the context of forgiveness, learning and joy in who we are and what we are called to do. As I have looked back, in so much of my life story, I have faced what seemed like unfair, even painful, relational situations. And yet my life has also been full of deep and rich relationships that have spurred me on and affirmed who I am and where I was going.

Kaleidoscope Reflections

- What do you have to celebrate from this historical vantage point?
- What are some of the successes you have experienced as a leader?

- How important is celebration to you as you seek to become the leader you want to be?

- Describe the people and the relationships that have been and may still be significant. Find ways to express your gratitude for who they are and what they have invested in you and your leadership journey.

- If this was the story of your life, to whom would you dedicate it, and why do they matter in your story?

For example: This question was not in my original Self-Leadership Pathway. It came over time and then the thought came suddenly as I visited with my dear friend Clara, to whom this book is dedicated. As I mentioned in the dedication, Clara is ninety-three and a wonderful woman of faith, ready to move on to her eternal home with Jesus. As Brian and I spent the day with her most recently, we were preparing to leave when she asked Brian to pray. He did. Clara then went on to say to us, "This is what I am telling my family and you are family to me. We have been family for a long time. I don't want any mourning. I'll be where I want to be." I could feel the tears welling up in my soul and in my eyes as Clara spoke. I knew what she was saying and yet, need I say more? I had known for a while, as Clara would express similar sentiments in our conversations on the phone at different times, that I did not want to let her go. And yet in the days previous to driving to her place in Banff, I knew I needed to let her know that I was willing to release her. As we got up to hug each other goodbye, I knew I needed to say that now. I managed to tell her that when Jesus came to say, "Clara, I want you with me," that although I didn't want to let her go, I would let her go. There were more hugs and tears were held back. We said goodbye. Brian and I were silent until we got our Starbucks drinks and went and sat on the patio in the sun. Brian said, "I have not seen Clara like this before." The well of tears was so present and pushing to overflow and yet we were able to talk. We were able to reminisce about the gift of love and a mother's heart that Clara had given, particularly to me and also to our family. We shared about the gift she had given me of time and space to come away to Banff, to her sanctuary and to write. Now it was becoming the book she always believed I could write. What a great opportunity to dedicate this volume of words from my heart to her.

Who has given you—what you might not have realized then—a gift that has contributed to who you are today?

4. *SCOR*

S: Strengths and Abilities

1. Take out any assessments you have completed over time and record what you discovered about yourself. Describe where you saw raw talent at that time and in retrospect how you would describe your growth as a leader. Are there any stagnant places you need to address?

2. Describe what made or makes your heart sing. What makes you put your head on the pillow at night with a sweet sigh of what a great day it was? It is not necessarily because everything went well. It is an acknowledgment that you lived true to your values and who you were created to be.

3. What do you sense people see and experience as your strengths?

4. Who do you have working with you who has strengths in areas you do not? Describe how you can deepen your work by combining those strengths.

5. How well do you work with those who have differing strengths? What might you need to learn to be more effective together even though you are different?

6. What is going to threaten your leadership in the organization if you do not take the time to see it or address it?

7. What are the factors that influence the leadership style you are exercising?

8. Write your philosophy of celebration in the workplace that you want to pursue. What values will guide you in living this philosophy?

> I remember a time when Ruth led our staff team through an exercise to discover and discuss our various strengths and abilities with one another. We were a mixture of pastors, coordinators, and administrative assistants, and our discussion revealed more of who each of us were as whole people, beyond our abilities within our staff role. We were surprised by some of the things we learned about one another, and even about ourselves, and we were encouraged by the affirmation we received from each other of the unique strengths and abilities that each of us brought to the team. But perhaps the greatest value was in the conversations over the following days. We started to see and tap into each other's strengths beyond the narrow confines of our roles: an administrative assistant was invited by a pastor to share strategic ideas, a pastor worked with an administrator to improve an important process, and a coordinator highlighted the importance of empathy in a difficult situation. We each still focused on our roles, but our work was enhanced by others' abilities and strengths. We also had a greater understanding of each other's weaknesses, and we could talk about them more openly with grace. In short, we enhanced each other's roles, and both the effectiveness of the ministry and the health of the team flourished. Knowing ourselves and one another better and affirming and drawing on each other's strengths were catalytic in our development as individuals and team.
>
> Greg Grunau

Discovering who you are is a lifetime journey. Don't ever forget that. The journey comes not just in what you find out about yourself in the moment of reading the assessments, it also comes in after discoveries and affirmations from others along the way. It comes as you discover things you did not know.

Many years ago I filled in an assessment tool that showed you how you worked best on a team. Some of the terms were, visionary, refiner, prototyper, pioneer, etc. Well, when I filled it in way back when, I already knew I was a visionary and so I lived and walked in that knowledge. One day, a long number of years later, in discussion with a faithful, longtime friend, as we were talking and I was drawing, he asked me if I had ever filled in that particular assessment. I said yes. He asked, "Of those terms what were you?" I said I am a visionary. He then said, "What was your second descriptor?" Hmm, I didn't know. I went home and pulled the assessment off the computer. Well, what a discovery! I was also a prototyper and the percentage score was only a 1% difference! Most of my adult life I had been teased about the pictures, the diagrams and the charts I drew. My kids would tease and say to others, "Talk, and Mom will turn it into a picture." I had struggled at times, as I didn't see a lot of other people do this and I did wonder about me. What a huge aha moment this was to me. It was who I was and had been and now all these years later, here was a new understanding about myself to be maximized.

C. Challenges

1. As you reflect back on the purple stickies, which were your leadership memories? Describe the painful, confusing, disappointing situations that happened.

2. How did it influence who you wanted to be as a leader or who you did not want to be as a leader?

3. Describe what you learned through these times.

4. What is going to threaten your leadership in the organization if you do not take the time to see or address this painful reality?

5. Write your philosophy of the challenging times in the workplace. What do you want to remember as you continue to navigate challenging times? What are the values that will guide you?

Whether we like it or not, our learnings come in many, many different ways. Challenges are the opportunities to draw on our inner resources, lean into our healthy relationships, reaffirm our values and find a way forward. These are the times when we realize how necessary it is to have relationships that we can lean into, accept wisdom from and apply what we are coming to know in deeper ways.

O. Opportunities

1. What are the opportunities you have been given and what have you learned about yourself as a leader in those opportunities?

2. What are the factors that influence the leadership style you are exercising?

3. How will you continue to be mindful or intentional in your leadership from your learnings?

When faced with opportunities we are wise to revisit our values, our strengths and our purposes. Every opportunity is not a call for an automatic yes. There are times that we may say yes and yet our yes may be for all the wrong reasons. Or it can be for the right reasons and yet it is not a forever yes. Reflection is key to healthy leadership. There are times when our yes or no are not that simple. Open doors are not necessarily the standard for saying yes. What we consider closed doors are not necessarily the standard for saying no. Our lives are so much deeper than the simplicity of how easy it looks.

I recall being offered a position that sounded like another one of my dreams come true. So, after much thought I said yes and so began a leadership journey that did not turn out at all the way I had perceived at the start. It held some hard lessons and yet those lessons have been rich and deep. They helped to mold and shape me for another part of my leadership journey with a free heart and not with a deep well of bitterness.

As I learned more about myself and reflected on who I was becoming, the decisions around those opportunities have become clear much sooner and much more readily. I have continued to be reminded of a universal principle I had learned before and now would learn again, that I always have choices. Choices are around where I choose to live my values, in my outlook and attitude, no matter how they turn out.

R: Roadblocks:

1. As you look at who you want to become or how you want to deepen your leadership, what do you sense your roadblocks are to becoming who you want to be?

2. Which of the roadblocks are from within, or are intrinsic?

3. What capacity do you have to move through these intrinsic roadblocks?

4. What is your approach where your capacity is static, in other words where it cannot change?

5. Which of the roadblocks are from without, or are extrinsic?

6. What capacity do you have to move through these extrinsic roadblocks?

7. What is your approach where your capacity is static?

A thought-provoking quote by American athlete, Michael Strahan says, *"We're our own worst enemy. You doubt yourself more than anybody else ever will. If you can get past that, you can be successful."* Roadblocks are for either moving or learning to move around. They can be stepping-stones to where we want to go when we see them as such, rather than doubting who we are or what we are capable of. The fact of the matter is we need each other to navigate the roadblocks whether real or perceived in our lives and our leadership.

I have had the privilege of working in the nonprofit sector for a number of years enabling the leaders there to hone their leadership skills. When I was first invited in, I said no. I turned the opportunity down because the biggest roadblock I saw in my way was my lack of a Master's Degree or a PhD. How could I waste the time of these great contributors to our society?

A year later I was invited in again. My thoughts on what I had to offer had shifted. I began to recognize the deficit in much of leadership development was around the soft skills of Emotional Intelligence. This was one of my greatest strengths. Some twelve years later, I sit where the privilege and responsibility to enable leaders to move forward comes readily. I not only understand my strengths, I know how to make them a positive energy in my leadership.

4. Capacity

Webster's dictionary says *capacity* is "1. **ability** to contain or deal with something. The room has a large seating **capacity**. Factories are working to **capacity**. 2. mental or physical power."

You have the capacity to do better. Capacity is an interesting concept with two contrasts. Think of capacity like a steel beam, that once a bridge is built of steel, it holds a very limited ability to expand or contract. It cannot afford to change dramatically or chaos would ensue as vehicles attempt to cross the bridge. This is the limit of what it can do. There is a stability and predictability to the capacity it has. Alternatively, think of capacity like the gas tank in your vehicle. It will only hold so much, you can't make it hold more; and when it is empty, it is empty and you cannot run a vehicle on an empty tank. The vehicle will only go as far as it has fuel to take it.

Static Capacity

What-if I began spending time and energy on where I had the most potential for growth?

 Kaleidoscope Reflections

1. How would you describe your limits as a leader? For example, consider limits like time, energy, resources, abilities, or skills.

2. Which of these limits are from your intrinsic beliefs about yourself and your leadership? Name them.

3. Which of these limits are from extrinsic sources? Name them.

4. What limitations do you need to work within, or it will mean disaster?

5. What kind of strengths do you need in the people that work with you in order to work to capacity?

One of the gifts of age is the recognition of what I can do really well and what I do not excel at. It is the wisdom to know what do I take on, and what I simply will entrust to someone else who does it better. I believe we do not do the younger generation well when we tell them, "Dream it and you can be anything you want to be." This is a myth of epic proportions that squanders resources like time, money, relationships. It doesn't matter how much I apply myself to learning technical skills on my computer (even though I have surprised myself at times at what I have learned). I have come to know beyond a shadow of a doubt that figuring technical matters out is not the way my brain is wired. And yet, I know some really great people with whom, when we can pull the best of what we do together, we can accomplish so much more. It means we can see our skills sets as complimentary rather than competitive. We also recognize we do not need to do it all. We can find others who will help to create a greater whole. Neither one of us is capable at excelling at what the other person is so excellent at.

In one of the organizations I worked at, I had an incredible staff team of eight people. One of my leadership strengths was helping my people, through a variety of ways, come to see what they do best. We found the exhilarating joy and achievement of learning to know ourselves better and seeking to understand those we worked with better, which truly built a dream team. This team never felt they had to do something better than anyone else on the team; they just needed to ask the expert in that area to step up and to make a difference together.

Adaptive Capacity

What-if I grasped the resources to maximize my limits both intrinsically and extrinsically in a life-giving way?

Think of capacity like a seed such as an acorn, when planted in the right conditions it will multiply its capacity exponentially. As a leader, knowing your own capacities will enable you to be a greater collaborator, influencer, and builder of teams. Take an honest look at yourself in order to maximize your strengths and lead through your challenges in a way that enhances the team, the project, the people, your leadership.

Some days are myth busters in my life. One of those days was a graduation for one of our executive cohorts. My co-facilitator and I shared the themes of all we had brought to the table for learning and discussion. Then each executive began to share the amazing stories of their learnings and aha moments they had experienced over the past six months. The inspiration was unstoppable. The heads and hearts that came to each one of these cohorts was amazing and so rich with wisdom. Safety, trust, relationship, focus and respect are a few of the values that keep us tracking together and moving forward.

There are times I think back to when I said no to this opportunity because of my huge prideful stance of self-doubt. Now I realize how rich my life has become since I changed that no to yes. I learned to bring the best of myself to the cohort and live in expectancy of each executive bringing the best of themselves. We have all adapted and grown and we see each other in new and fresh ways, amazed at who we are becoming.

 Kaleidoscope Reflections

1. What does it feel and look like when your tank is full, and you are leading at the best you have to offer?

2. What does it look and feel like when you are trying to lead on empty?

3. Think of capacity like an acorn, which becomes a mighty oak tree. What areas of growth lie within you? Describe them. Reflect on how you could cause them to increase in effectiveness.

Whether you are reflecting on static or adaptive capacity, the language you use around those concepts is either life-giving or limiting. There are times in our leadership growth journey that we need to adopt new or fresh language in order to enable ourselves to move forward.

For example: It seems in the past number of years—as our culture has lived on adrenaline, sought adventure, been pressed for time—leaders have coined the term *best practices*. The desire has been to find the fixes that will enable us to keep moving at breakneck speed and not have to reinvent the wheel. This term has definitely become a trigger for me as I have seen best practices that work in one organization create chaos in another organization.

Recently in a board meeting one of the members introduced the term *leading practices*. I found I resonated with that term. To me it gave the freedom to look at all kinds of practices in order to reflect on what and where I was leading. Then I could work through those practices until I came to the ones that were in sync with my organization. This would allow me to lead others to find the leading practices for their organizations. This would be adaptive capacity at its best. For me the term *best practices* brought up an inner resistance in me that was limiting. The term *leading practices* energized me. It was life-giving and allowed me to think inside and outside the box to a forward moving outcome.

 Kaleidoscope Reflections

1. How would you describe the capacity you have to live in the THERE that you are describing?

2. Where can you push forward and where do you need to scale back your expectations?

3. What language are you using that is creating unrealistic pressure and stress on who you want to be?

4. How could you change or reframe the language you are using for a more positive outcome?

It is not unusual for me to pay attention to my language to see if it is reflecting a scarcity mindset or a realistically optimistic abundant mindset. In a recent decision I had been contemplating, I recognized that I had gotten very black and white in my considerations. My language began to reflect that with words like, "I can't…" or, "They will have to…" This was very limiting to any kind of innovation or creativity. I began to shift my language by making myself think about potential choices I had not considered yet. They didn't necessarily have to be viable choices, just the fact that there were choices allowed me to be more open in my considerations. It also brought a sense of relief. I was not boxed in or being forced into a one size fits all answer.

Notes—record your most significant thoughts to reflect on and to begin bold action.

Chapter 10
Quadrant 3, ACQUIRE

What-if I approached relationships and resources as gifts to be used for the greater good?

Through the previous exercises you have come to understand yourself, your hopes and dreams, your values in fresh and meaningful ways.

Now that you have reflected on:

INSPIRE—your new THERE

- Who do you want to be as a leader?

- Why does that matter?

- What do you want to do?

ANALYZE—HERE

What your current reality is based on:

- your history

- what you have to celebrate

- Your SCOR—strengths, challenges, opportunities, and roadblocks

- What your capacity is both static and adaptive

You now have a base from which to move forward in your ongoing development as a leader to look at what you will need to **ACQUIRE** to keep moving forward.

Who Do You Need

What-if you had a dream team of all the people who hold all the strengths and abilities you know are needed to do what is needed with excellence?

Our relationships are key to our success as leaders. Who do you need in your life who will be like iron sharpening iron? These are the key relationships that have an authentic give and take. They are the relationships that ground us, that keep us aware of our strengths and our vulnerabilities. They are the people who are willing to walk the long haul with us.

 ## Kaleidoscope Reflections

1. Name which relationships drain you and deplete your energy and how you handle these.

2. Name the relationships that energize you. How often are you active within these relationships?

We do not experience relationships on an equal continuum. E. T. Hall coined the phrase *proxemics* which he defined as, "the branch of knowledge that deals with the amount of space that people feel it necessary to set between themselves and others."

Joseph Meyers goes on to explain proxemics more clearly in his book, *Search to Belong*, which speaks to four spaces where we can have a sense of belonging:

Public Space

When we are drawn together by influences or common interests outside of ourselves, we have a sense of belonging, or I fit here. It is not about individuals connecting person to person, it is based on sharing common experiences together. "Think of fans at a football game, members of a Parent Teacher Association," a motorcycle crew, shoppers at a grocery store, an art class, a book club. In each case an outside influence brings us into a common space.

We may not even know each other; you might say we are strangers to each other. If we have a sense of "we belong here" we move from being a stranger to becoming an insider, we belong. In this kind of relational space, we know very little about each other, in fact we have little to no personal information from the person standing right beside us as our focus is what brought us into this context. If we sense, we belong we begin to look at what it would mean to participate in some way that is significant for us. When we feel like we belong it moves us beyond just being together - we share a common bond.

Social Space

Inconsequential conversations are where we move into social space. We begin to step out and share snippets of information about ourselves in order to see how we are received. We seek to make great first impressions and see where that might lead.

"Take away social relationships and our community conversation becomes flat, lacking a spontaneous connection to the entirety of our relationships. Social belonging is the space where we connect through sharing 'snapshots' of who we are. Such phrases as first impressions and best foot forward refer to this type of spatial belonging."

"Social space is important:

1. It provides space for neighbour relationships." A neighbour is someone you know well

enough to ask for small favours—to walk the dog, or pick up the mail. These relationships bring to the neighbourhood—safety, comfort and connectedness.

2. "Social space is a safe selection space for us to decide with whom we would like to grow deeper." We gather the kind of information that helps us make that decision.

3. This space allows interactions that allow us to display a reality we create around who we really are, while at the same time enabling others to witness a sample of the processes through which this reality was created over months and years.

4. We all play various roles and in social space we measure what we will let others know about who we are or what we do."

Have you ever heard people say to you, "I didn't know that about you?"

When we answer the person who asks what we do, we may ask inside our head, "What would make the most sense for this person to know about me?"

Personal Space

"These are the people that no matter how long you are apart when you get together it is like you have never been apart.

You share private information. We both know this information is in safe keeping.

Personal space is where we connect through sharing private, although not naked experiences, thoughts and feelings.

We call these people our 'close friends.'"

Intimate Space

"In intimate space we share naked experiences, feelings and thoughts. Intimate relationships are those in which another person knows the "naked truth" about us and yet the two of us are not ashamed. Intimacy is based on the definition of "nakedness" and "ashamed." "Nakedness" is not just physical, it is also emotional, informational and spatial. "Ashamed" does not mean embarrassed. Embarrassment does not necessarily mean shame. Shame is the experience of the intimate self, exposed in inappropriate ways."

In my pastoral journey in public ministry this was a learning curve for me. Although gifted with a pastoral heart, when I stepped into pastoring as a role, I had no idea how relationally challenging that would be. Over the years I had had many deep and meaningful relationships. I learned that in any relationship each person is a part of determining the level of relationship. One of my misconceptions of pastoring was, wasn't I to be able to meet the people in front of me and bring a heart of caring and compassion? Well, that was true and yet to be healthy and effective it had to have a framework.

I discovered that it did not matter which leadership role I held. I could use this *Search to Belong* framework and it still applied. I was able to learn healthy ways of making it work well.

"These are the people that no matter how long you are apart when you get together it is like you have never been apart. You share private information. We both know this information is in safe keeping.

In leadership you soon learn that people desire relationship with you for a wide variety of reasons. Without a framework to guide you, relational situations can arise that will make you question your leadership abilities and leave you vulnerable to unnecessary relational pain.

I learned to be a relationally healthy leader who could meet people as they came to me and relate to them on relationally acceptable levels. This did not always please those who wanted more from me than I was prepared to give, and yet my values gave me a framework to know how to handle those situations in a life-giving way. I could fully embrace the situation without compromising my relational values.

Our lives revolve around relationships of all kinds. We were made for relationship. As leaders, we often hear about how lonely it is to be a leader. It is freeing to realize that we don't have to be a victim to loneliness. We can take the responsibility to feed our relational sides as well as our minds and bodies. One tool that has helped me develop healthy relationships has definitely been the framework of relational spaces and the values around them, as well as the Relational Web.

Relational Web Exercise

What-if I learned to lead through relationships in a life-giving way?

The purpose of this exercise is to take a quick inventory of the kind of positive or negative energy you are experiencing in your relationships.

The Relational Web

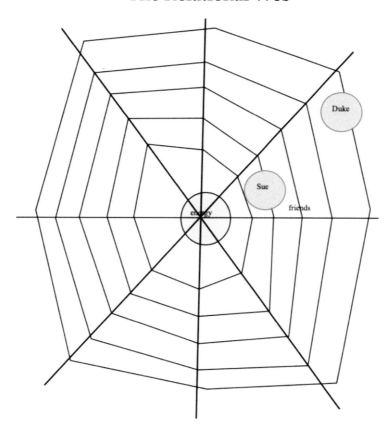

 Kaleidoscope Reflections

1. What do you want more of in your relationships?

2. What do you want less of in your relationships?

3. Take each individual relationship and ask yourself, "What is my part of the relationship that needs work?"

4. What is the other person's part of the relationship that needs work?

5. Each line represents a relational theme such as friends, family, colleagues, supervisor, direct report, mentors, etc. As you look at your life, what terms would you give to the relationships you presently have? Put one of those terms on a line.

6. Now make a list of the people that fit in those relational description terms.

   At the centre of the web is a circle named energy. This represents the greatest source of positive energy in your relationships. The farther away from the centre means the less energy you get from that relationship.

7. Take one name and draw a circle on the web that represents the relational term and how much energy you sense you receive from that relationship. If you receive a lot of energy

from that relationship, then place the circle and name close to the centre. If you do not receive so much positive energy from a relationship put it on the line to indicate that.

8. Note what you are feeling as you scan the web.

9. How many and which relationships energize you? Describe what that looks like and feels like.

10. How many and which relationships drain you? Describe what that looks like and feels like.

11. Which of the relationships are or have the potential for giving you feedback and sharing perspective with you in a life-giving way?

12. In which relationships would it be appropriate and beneficial to ask the following questions?

    a. What do you want to celebrate about me?
    b. What do you want to caution me about?

13. Do any of the relationships have issues that need to be addressed and put to rest?

14. Which relationships need your attention right now and what kind of attention do they need? Example: Sue is a friend and is someone you find energizes you quite a bit. Duke is a friend and yet you find your energy being diminished when you spend time with him.

15. Now that you have completed the Relational Web, what are your observations you want to begin to address in light of who you have said you want to be as a leader and why that matters?

16. Indicate who and what you will do, what is the timeline and where will this fit on your calendar.

17. What is your intrinsic inspiration to keep working at this and who or what might you need for extrinsic inspiration to keep moving forward?

What Do You Need?

Once again, as you look to who you want to be as a leader in this next season of your life, what are the resources such as money, facility, education, materials, tools, etc.?

For example:

As I left pastoring in a large church to work more in a leadership development area with others, I was not totally clear on what all I needed. As I answered a lot of these questions in the light of who I wanted to be in this next season of leadership, I found people affirming me in the area of emotional intelligence. I found myself intrigued by it and although I had begun reading about it years earlier, I decided to take a number of courses to increase my knowledge and also to grow in my own emotional intelligence. I then mapped out who I would take the training from, where would I travel to take it, what was the timeframe and how did this fit on my calendar. I also looked at what would be the financial cost for this training. What parts of my present life needed to be rearranged and considered in order to take this training? I created and defined my strategic intentions. Then I looked at how I would move towards accomplishing them. As these realities were addressed, I found my excitement and inspiration at what I would do growing and gaining greater clarity.

 ## Kaleidoscope Reflections

Who are your confidants?

"They usually operate apart from your organizations boundary, although occasionally someone very close in whose interests are perfectly aligned with yours, can also play the role. Confidants can provide you with a place where you can say anything that's in your heart, everything that is on your mind, without being pre-digested or well packaged."
Leadership on the Line, Heifetz and Linsky

1. What talents, abilities etc. do you need in others to strengthen your leadership and your effectiveness?

2. Who are your confidants? Confidants have few, if any conflicting loyalties. They have your back.

3. In what ways are you pursuing healthy relationships with your allies?

Who are your allies?

"Allies are the people who share many of your values, or at least your strategy, and operate across some organizational or factional boundary. Their first loyalty is to the organization not necessarily to you."
Leadership on the Line, Heifetz and Linsky

1. Who are the people who believe in you and also have the organization's best interests in mind?

2. What depth of relationship do you need to pursue with them?

3. What would be the cautions for these relationships and why does that matter?

You need both allies and confidants and also need to be able to differentiate each role in your life. Confidants are there when you need them most; their loyalty is to you. It is not a blind loyalty, but a loyalty that is realistic and focuses on the conversations of concern with you first of all and not with many others.

Allies have a loyalty to you, and yet their belief and loyalty to the organization will supersede their loyalty to you. They are wonderful people to have in your life to help you see beyond yourself. They will be the reminder of what the organization is about and why that matters.

Notes—record your most significant thoughts to reflect on and to begin bold action.

Chapter 11

Quadrant 4, ACT

What-if my behaviours were a reflection of what I say I value?

As we come to this last quadrant called ACT, we are faced with making all that we have discovered and all that we hoped to be actionable. We will look at a number of focuses that will create the environment for success long term such as:

- how we lead ourselves in the use of our daily time
- our planning ahead
- our ability to invest in others

Focus

As you have worked through who you need and what you need, you now come to the place of naming the various focuses this will take and prioritize how and when you will approach each one.

As I looked at becoming more involved in leadership development on a larger scale, I took in all the considerations above. I was able to see my need to focus on four areas.

1. Rest

I had not realized how weary I had become. I realized a medical conversation with my doctor and a way to address my freshly named exhaustion was important to move forward. This meant a new focus on eating habits, exercise, what rest meant, and I fully gave myself permission to pursue this fresh lifestyle.

The fact that I had previously been able to rise at 5:00 a.m., work all day and fall into bed late and still have energy, had now changed. I had been living on adrenaline, which was now dropping quickly, and I felt like I would never be a functioning leader again. I was a bear with very little brain just like Winnie the Pooh! As I learned to give myself permission to change my former lifestyle, I found I could function with a new clarity that was not adrenaline dependent. I found I was even more values driven and free to know when it was good to say yes and when it was good to say no. I began to pay attention to what meaningful rest looked like for me and to schedule it into my calendar. I became proactive in order to experience sustainable leadership.

2. Relationships

I had always had strong and vibrant relationships. As I became more in tune with who I was to be in this leadership season, I also became more aware of the kinds of relationships I needed for my growth and the kind of relationships I needed to breathe life into. The Relational Web was one of the tools that was helpful.

3. Input

I was eager and hungry for more education, and yet not for the sake of knowledge. It was for the sake of increasing who I was as a person. This then affected the overflow of my life as I walked with others to become all they were intended to be. I had always been an avid reader. I was now a more selective reader. I had always loved taking courses, workshops, etc., and now I found I was more selective in what I spent my time on.

What had changed? Previously going at full tilt as much as possible was fun. It also had the side benefit of a certain kind of status. Now my focus was growth. I learned to ask myself:

- How would this book, this course, this material, or this workshop, increase who I was as a leader in what I had to offer to others?

- How did it change me and my lifestyle first of all, so that I was not telling others what they should do? I was now listening in deeper ways and learning to ask great questions for them to address in their journey. I was able time and again as appropriate to share my journey, the ups, the downs, the doubts, the fears, the joys, the sorrows in a much more realistic and inspiring way.

As you work through finding your focus some of the things you discover may be the same and some will be unique to you. Keep asking yourself the curious questions. This will enable you to become all you were created to be, not in order to become what someone else became and thinks you should become.

What-if you were able to embrace ways to spend your time that actually creates a space for healthy priorities and rhythms in life and leadership?

Time: navigating the context of calendar

You may have heard of this concept as time management, or life management, or work/life balance. These are all descriptive terms that failed to resonate with me for several reasons. Managing my time did not make me the most effective. I had a heart condition that determined how productive I could be based on my energy levels, not on the time available. Life management made me resent the concept of being managed. In my leadership philosophy, tasks are managed, and people are led. I had seen the damage and shame associated with the concept of work/life balance and considered it a myth to be dispelled. The concept of balance creates guilt, avoidance and a nonproductive life. Why? Because we can never achieve the balance that we are told is the right balance. I preferred the concept of life leadership. I am responsible to figure out how I can maximize not just my time, but also my energy in order to live with the purpose I was made for.

Because I was taught from the Bible from an early age, I was intrigued to see how Jesus handled work/life balance. I began to read Bible stories about Jesus with leadership eyes. To my immense relief and encouragement, His life unfolded in rhythms. I recorded those rhythms and loved what I saw. He worked hard doing the work and developing relationships, and then He would go off on His own. God was literally His Father and also His boss. So, He pulled aside to be alone and to also consult with His boss and His Father. Then He would go back into the thick of His work only to pull aside again when the need was there. Life leadership gives you the space to create a life with healthy rhythms in order to go the long haul.

Living by what Jesus valued most seemed to be His way. Our values are a part of our story as well. We started with defining them in Section 1, Inspiration. Values are crucial to knowing what we base our decisions on. Values give us the courage and wisdom to know when to say yes and when to say no. Values also allow us to deal with conflict, based on the issues rather than taking the conflict personally and getting stuck in the hurt feelings conflict has the potential to produce.

As we focus on what we value most in life, interruptions will be a constant surge of irritation. Having a values-inspired life allows for being who we were created to be and getting to our THERE, where we want to be. We can finish what we start and leave space for the unexpected. This also allows space for the interruptions, while becoming better people and leaders in the process.

What-if the interruptions we face in life were about developing and enlarging our character, helping us understand what we truly say we value and how we choose to live?

As I was working on this manuscript, I decided to check my emails. One email was from an editor friend who had such a massive headache that screen time was out of the question for her. An interruption! I picked up another email that held an apology for not getting back to me because of a death in the family. An interruption! Both scenarios held interruptions that stopped the activities each one of those leaders would have determined were important that day. Our challenge is to live in spite of the interruptions that hover around us. Our challenge is to be in tune enough with the rhythms we are pursuing to not allow them to defeat us in the moment. It often is the little things that take away our inner quiet. These include the shoddily completed work that is turned in late, the appointment that shows up half an hour late, or worse yet doesn't show, or any other situation that create stress for you when you are interrupted. The way we order our lives impacts our sense of fulfillment, our success, and our ability to handle interruptions.

The word balance is a word that usually catches my attention. It is a word that is meaningful in justice and in pricing by weight. In life leadership the idea of balance creates an environment for a sense of failure and defeat. Organization and life leadership look different for different people. There are some significant principles that when understood and applied in your life can result in inner peace and reduce stress.

An interesting fact is that there never has been anything but a twenty-four hour a day, a seven day a week and a fifty-two week a year. Oh yes, there are always exceptions that prove the rule, like February! And yet what we do with the time we have been given is our individual choice. So, let's consider some important principles to guide us.

Early on as a young adult, I sat under the teaching on time management by Stephen Covey. It shaped my life powerfully and has served me well to be able to live beyond guilt and shame. It also created a space for me to figure out what worked best for me in the roles I fulfilled. Our days are numbered and yet we have the choice of how we use our time. My personal story of death, sickness, drunk drivers, loss, grief and mourning made learning rhythms of life a positive and needful choice. Watching how leaders I admired (and also those I did not admire) used their time fascinated me. In my early years away from home, I met many leaders who were so passionate about what they did, and yet they held a twisted mantra that sounded something like this:

I so love what I do that I want to burn out doing it!

There was even a time in my years serving in the church when I thought that sounded so noble, until my hubby looked at me and asked, "If you burn out doing what you love, what use will you be?" Reality check! I will say in the heat of exhaustion that was a tough question. And yet I came to learn a more fulfilling and effective way to lead myself and manage my energy through the rhythms of time, life, health and well-being.

In Section 1 we looked at how values are a key determining factor of how we use our time and why that matters. We will keep those principles in mind as we move through this material.

We will consider three key time use concepts expressed in metaphors as we look at our work as leaders:

1. The dance floor where we spend the bulk of our time.

2. The balcony, which gives us a thirty thousand-foot or fifty thousand-foot view.

3. The window seat which reshapes and renews our inner view.

In any new project or situation, theoretically our time usage all makes sense until we get into the fire of actually making it work for us. Determining what healthy rhythms are for each of us will free us to live in abundance. A scarcity of time will tend to make us grumpy, impatient and less than we can be.

Just to get a glimpse of what your life entails, consider the following visual exercise.

Kaleidoscope Reflections

As you consider the above table setting, fill in the following information.

1. **Dinner Plate**

   Note all the things you presently have on your plate.

2. **Bread and Butter Plate**

   Note the areas of your life you probably do without thinking but are significant and necessary.

3. **Knife**

   What do you sense you need to cut out of your life right now?

4. **Fork**

   Note the things you would like to dig a little deeper into and understand at a greater depth.

5. **Spoon**

   Note the things or areas where you sense you could use more help, such as a mentoring or coaching relationship, a learning opportunity, administrative or organizational help, even another hire.

6. **Dessert Plate**

   Note the things you are doing that are fun for you, that lie outside work and responsibility.

7. **Water Glass**

   Note the things you have done in the last month that you can say have filled you up.

8. Napkin

Note what you have in place that protects and provides for you physically, mentally, spiritually and emotionally.

• Having completed this exercise what are your observations about your present lifestyle and the rhythms that you pursue?

• What is one area that stands out to you where you may need to:

STOP–REFLECT–RECALCULATE

• What will you do and who will you ask to hold you accountable?

What-if you discovered the rhythms of work and life that allowed you to be focused, adaptable and thriving in a culture of accountability?

As I have worked with executives in the ministry world, nonprofit world and the business world, one common trend I hear about and see is the ambiguity around what fills them up, what is fun and what provides for them or protects them. They are excellent at filling the dinner plate to overflowing! Depending on how long they have filled the dinner plate to overflowing and neglected the dessert plate, glass and napkin, influences the amount of joy and productivity they find in each day.

I so love the metaphor of the dailiness of life being like a dance floor. It lends credence to a number of things:

• the work it takes to learn how to dance and execute the dance moves well
• the fun that music and movement bring as we move within the parameters given
• the bump-ups that can annoy and even harm us

As we dance, we see what is right around us, which may be quite a bit or it can be very limited depending how oriented we are to paying attention. When we see what is right around us, we become limited in remembering the bigger picture, the vision of where we want to be and go.

This means we can get caught up in the minutia and even think it is the main thing because it looks pretty big right under our noses. We find ourselves expending our energy in ways that may not best reflect what is expected of us. The dance floor is about the tasks, the people, the schedules, the rules of engagement, the paperwork, the social media, all the demands that are right beside or in front of us. Leadership requires larger views and broader understandings.

There are two views that you cannot afford to miss if you want long-term sustainability, fulfillment, and effectiveness:

The Balcony

The Balcony is a metaphor for seeing other views, appreciating differing perspectives, or having different vantage points. The balcony is about stepping up to see from a higher perspective. It is moving from looking at the individual to looking at the whole dance floor. The perspective is so different and can be changed again when we give the kaleidoscope a twist. That twist leaves a new impression.

To look from the balcony requires having clarity about where we are going and the overview of where, why, what, who and when. This is the wide sweeping strokes of our framework.

For example, in the executive leadership world we talk about "Six Things the ED or CEO Holds" as written by Corey Olynik. This is about executive leadership where the Executive Director or CEO is responsible for the bottom line on all these topics and yet is not responsible to do each one. They are responsible to see that the responsibilities of execution lie with the right person in the right role.

The balcony view in this example would be:

1. *Vision/Values*: The ED/CEO takes the lead in how and when these are set and with whom. They also lead in keeping them alive.

2. *Strategy/Execution*: The ED/CEO takes the lead in what, how, when, who and why this is created, communicated and kept alive.

3. *Quality/Service Excellence*: Out of the strategy the ED/CEO entrusts this to their staff and volunteers with clear expectations, empowerment, communication and accountability

4. *People/Culture*: The ED/CEO sets and leads the working environment and culture. They get the behaviour they put up with.

5. *Money coming and going*: The ED/CEO can hire for raising money; they can't give up responsibility for what happens to the money.

6. *The Story, Internal/External*: The ED/CEO is the chief storyteller and is responsible for the story to align inside and outside the organization.

 Kaleidoscope Reflections

1. What kind of time frame would be reasonable for you and how often would you need it to begin creating a fuller picture from a balcony perspective?

2. Create the plan.

3. Set a time for Balcony on your calendar to reflect on the bigger picture and to keep your head above the details. Find a rhythm that works for you and keep it alive.

The Window Seat

The home I presently live in has been our family home since 1985. The upper floor has a wondrous view of the city of Calgary. That view holds much significance for me in the work I do. While Brian and I were away traveling with Rocky Mountain College Choir, our family and some dear friends remodeled our bedroom with a window seat as the focus. They built a beautiful floor to ceiling cabinet with a window seat for me. What a gift! That window seat has been a place of reflection, renewal, visioning, imagining and strategizing. The window seat is the picture of making time to think, away from all the distractions, interruptions and demands, in order to ponder and reflect on those things that fill me up and renew my mind and heart for the purpose I am called to.

The first Monday of each month is given to Balcony time, taking the thirty thousand to fifty-thousand foot view of my world. The fourth Monday of the month is spent in my window seat, reflecting on myself as a whole person. I then look at what needs to be affirmed and what needs some tweaking. My journal is a key tool for this day as I consider the past month and also the path ahead. The time frame and frequency are not sacred. Find the rhythm that works best for you. Start small and grow. This will prevent biting off too much and then being discouraged that it does not work. A key principle in life management is that the time you take to plan and also to reflect, will make your life more productive and meaningful in all areas.

All three metaphors—the dance floor, the balcony and the window seat—are major components of the rhythms to focus your life leadership on.

 Kaleidoscope Questions

1. Determine what would make reasonable rhythms for you. How much time are you giving to your role at work? Is it what it should be? How often do you need to put a balcony day on your calendar in order to see what you are missing in the dailiness of life and work? Or how often do you need a window seat day that keeps you connected to your essence, your values, what you say is important to you?

2. How do you sense the pressure shift when you speak of rhythms which ebb and flow versus balance that is about right or wrong?

Notes—record your most significant thoughts to reflect on and to begin bold action.

Chapter 12

Calendar Mastery

What-if you became the master of your calendar and life gave you the sense that you could breathe each day?

We have looked at life management and rhythms of living. This next section is one way to handle your calendar. It is the system I have developed for myself as a visual learner and as someone who loves the tangible feel of paper and pen. The same concept can be translated to digital as well. In the seventies, I designed and produced a Life Reflections Planner. In the process of designing it, developing a seminar to go with it, and marketing it, I gained a whole lot of education on many different levels. All of them were not necessarily financially viable and yet they were invaluable. Take what is useful for you from this section and if you already have a meaningful way of handling your calendar, then stick with that.

Calendar

The balcony view in the context of calendar would be a yearly rhythm. As Stephen Covey says, these are the big rock days. Often the big picture of seasons will also govern the time choices we make. For example, let's take vacation days: If you love the warmth, perhaps a vacation is placed in the middle of a cold winter when you plan to head to warmer places. If your family is grown, perhaps you take vacation based on when family holiday times are over, and the traffic has lessened. Perhaps you are given parameters by your organization as to what windows of time are available for vacation days. Perhaps vacation days are booked when you can work on the renovations. There are so many factors to consider. Take the time to figure out what are the defining concepts for each part of your life.

Balcony starts with looking at a yearly overview, which will set the pattern to follow:

- A quarterly review
- A monthly review and plan
- A weekly review and plan
- A daily reminder

Balcony also looks at how your values will influence the choices of how you spend your time. For example, as a leader my key value is inspire. How does that affect my calendar? It means I need to consider what the factors are that contribute to my ability to be inspiring.

 Kaleidoscope Reflections

Gather your supplies:

- Yearly calendar, a monthly calendar, and then decide if a weekly view and/or a daily view are most helpful for you.

- Bring the tool that allows you to track tasks.

- Coloured pens or pencils (optional)

- Values Cards

- A yearly calendar from work

- A family yearly calendar

One of the big rocks of a leader is finding the tools that enable us to maximize how we will use the calendar. This will empower us to do what we are created to be and do. As a visual person, coloured pens or pencils help me to see at a glance what the rhythms of my life look like. That may not resonate with you. Find what will make the calendar a useful tool in your leadership, rather than a hammer that drains your energy.

Yearly Calendar

You can download year at a glance calendars or purchase a blank monthly calendar for a given year. You can also use the calendar on your phone. I use a paper calendar as I love working with paper, pencil and pen, which evidences my handwriting and doodling. What I talk about below is universal no matter what calendar you use and yet the nuances will be particular to a paper and pencil set up.

I use a year at a glance for my initial planning, using a pencil for all entries. Later on, I colour coded with coloured mechanical pencils and each colour has a code that I relate to. This gives me the ability to see at a glance what the rhythms of my life are looking like. Turquoise is the colour I use for vacations, statutory holidays, and days off. In planning, the turquoise reminds me of my need to pay attention to time off. In reviewing it helps me understand what kind of a rest and renewal pattern I have in the overview of a week, or a month, or a year. Time off is hard to make sense of weekly. It is rather like a bank account: the longer the period of time the graph represents, the clearer the financial picture becomes. I do not like when I see a financial deficit one month and yet over the time frame of a year it can end up looking very healthy. So too in our calendars a week can be intense, fulfilling, and draining all at the same time. As a consistent pattern, that would not be healthy. When you look at the overview of year, you will see patterns of intensity, or of slower pace, or of restful times. You can also use a code much like Bullet Journaling does. I recommend Ryder Carols' *The Bullet Journal Method*, Stephen Covey's *Life Management*, and Lisa Morgan's *Organizing from the Inside Out*.

January to December is our calendar year and that may work well for many of you. For others, the rhythms of the year unfold September to June. Choose whichever makes the most sense to you.

The big picture of your calendar means taking time away from the dance floor. Calendar work on the dance floor is merely checking in to see what is coming next, when and what you need for that particular entry. The interruptions on the dance floor are distracting and keep your head down in the details, rather than looking back to review and looking up to see what lies ahead. Being strategic about your calendar is big picture calendar work. This is the start to your balcony day.

Only once a year do you have to spend the time to create the whole year. After that, your monthly calendar times are about considering the past month, the next month and a brief review of the next three to four months that lie ahead. Once you begin this rhythm, much of it becomes intuitive based on past experience.

Considering a Yearly Calendar

These are the following entries you need to consider:

- Work rhythms—have a copy of your work calendar to consult. If you have annual events that require your presence they need to be reflected on your calendar. Perhaps you have a fund-raising gala each year at the same time. Be sure and put that on the calendar. Perhaps you have Staff Development days—note these.

- Statutory Holidays—note these

- Fifth-week days of each month—wherever there are days that spill over into a fifth week, that is a great time to consider balcony days and/or window seat days. They do not have regular occurrences, as they are different every month.

- Vacation days, days off—note these

- Celebration times—birthdays, anniversaries etc. These will happen whether you pay attention or not.

- Family times—this will be interpreted into your context of family. Family with little children, with teenagers, with empty nest—all have very different demands. If you are single, or a couple, or grandparents, your context will shift. The interesting thing is that the context of our lives is never static; paying attention through balcony time is important.

- Volunteer Opportunities—this would include faith-based commitments, neighbourhood involvement and any other nonmandatory involvements.

- Entertainment or social occasions

- Others that are particular to you.

Quarterly Calendar

Once a quarter place balcony time on the calendar. This is not as intensive a check in as the yearly calendar.

- If you used colour coding on your calendar, what are you observing from just the colours that are showing up on your quarterly calendar? What is too little? Too much? Just right?

- Lay out the values that you say are important to you. Where do you see them appearing on your calendar? They are the measuring stick for what you say yes or no to. This reveals how integrated you are.

- This is your time to read through your weekly reviews, which you will learn about next.

- Check for completions, forgotten, or partially finished projects and decide what to do with them. You can reschedule or delete them.

- Decide if they are completed, even though perhaps not in a way you previously had planned. Is there anything that has been neglected that needs to be finished up?

- What were your major learnings and is there anything to do with those at this point?

- What needs to be added in light of the next three months, or what needs to be shifted in importance?

- Be sure all regular appointments and/or events are on their appropriate date and time with necessary information.

Monthly Calendar

For me the first Monday morning of every month is Balcony Day as described earlier. It is a time to renew perspectives, to step back to the big picture, to get my head out of the details. The last Monday of each month is my Window Seat Day, which is when I shut off my phone, read something that engages my mind and heart in a way that inspires me. As a woman of faith, I learned to do this at an early age. Whether you pursue a faith journey or not, this is a time to be engaged and inspired once more by what keeps your mind and heart whole and renewed.

Where are you drinking deeply from the wells of all that is good, whole and inspiring?

What is filling you and creating an abundance mindset that spills over onto those you lead?

What is needed on your calendar to keep you in a healthy space in the coming month? Do you have down time, or vacation, or days off or (name what fills you up)?

 Kaleidoscope Reflections

1. What are the activities that fill you up? Name them and be sure they are on your calendar.

2. What are meaningful vacations and what is your plan for the coming year? Approximate what each will cost.

Weekly Calendar

At the end of each week, take the time to go through your calendar and fill in the review page. Note activities, what was done, not done, what values you see revealed. Are there any shifts, changes, deletions, or additions? Are there any leads that will serve you well into the future? Are there any questions that need to be answered and when will you put that on the calendar and with whom?

How did the week add up to your top value and is there anything you need to address through appreciation, acknowledgement, or course correction needed? Where does that action go on your calendar? Look ahead at your next week and complete your to-do list for the coming week.

Daily Calendar

The night previous, look at the next day in order to be prepared for what is already planned. Make space for what you do not know. Put whatever materials you need to have the next day together, so all is ready for the morning.

You will see that the longest commitment to time is your Yearly Planning Day. Your least amount of time is your daily preparation. This is not about the right formula. It is about a recipe for success that fits you.

Kaleidoscope Reflections

1. How would you analyze and describe the way you approach your use of your time and resources?

2. Describe how this is moving you forward.

3. Describe where you are recognizing gaps.

4. Determine where you need to add some margin. Margin is about the spaces on our calendar that we create to allow for the unexpected and those things we have no power to control.

5. Take a moment to define how your thinking is shifting and what needed actions are being revealed.

Adaptability

Adaptability is "the quality of being able to adjust to new conditions" and/or "the capacity to be modified for a new use or purpose."

Adaptability requires the capacity to be resilient by learning to embrace an abundance mindset, to see the long game, to understand oneself in the midst of change and to understand human nature.

Resiliency

The definition of failure is a lack of resilience. We truly only fail when we cannot do the work or choose not to get back up and try again no matter how painful it may be. This means we have a character and spirit that is empowered to move beyond personal slights and hurts and embrace the choice to take the road less traveled.

Who has not failed? We read inspiring stories of great men and women who were confident and knew their purpose. Some of them thrived and some of them failed. What made the difference? Here are some thoughts on developing resilience:

1. **Ongoing development of emotional intelligence**

   The ongoing development of understanding oneself and understanding others leads to healthy leadership of yourself and in the relationships that are important to you.

2. **Healthy self-talk**

   This is the skill to understand the power that emotion has to redirect our self-talk and leads us to healthy decisions that move us forward. It is the skill to believe that negative self-talk diminishes us or leaves us defeated. Never believe everything you think; measure it against truth.

3. **Abundance mindset**

   This is learning to see the world and decisions we make from an abundance mindset, which says there is more than enough for all. It involves taking to task the scarcity mindset where resources never measure up to our wants. Scarcity comes from a fear base and abundance comes from a base of gratitude.

4. **The ability to believe the best of people and be prepare for less than the than the best.**

   Oh the people that come to mind that believed the best in us and set the stage for us to gain confidence and competence in who we are and what we could do! They are still the leaders I admire and respect. I'll never forget one particular leader who was interviewing my husband and me for a key volunteer role. He told us what he saw in us that would bring strength to our leadership influence and he also cautioned us about what he felt would diminish our leadership influence if we did not pay attention. I call it "the arm around the shoulder and the kick in the pants" form of mentoring! I loved it. It was honesty with grace.

5. **A call to something so much bigger than themselves**

   A resilient leader has discovered their purpose in a call that is so much bigger than themselves. They have a confidence that is not egocentric.

6. A willingness to learn from every endeavor.

Lifelong learning is a catchy phrase to throw around and yet is a much harder principle to fully live out. It is the willingness to look at any situation no matter how it turns out and to see with clarity what there is for us to learn. It is the ability to see and use the shift of the kaleidoscope.

7. They are selective of who they allow to speak into their lives and whose lives they speak into.

Resilient leaders choose carefully who they allow to speak into their lives. They are discerning about who will make a difference in moving them closer to accomplishing their purpose. They also note who may hinder or diminish their leadership influence. They also choose to work with those whose outlooks are willing and ready to learn and move forward. They choose where to invest their people energy.

We discussed adaptability in the light of capacity under the quadrant on ANALYZE. This adaptability is similar and yet different. As you look at who you want to become as a leader in this season of life, you will find yourself becoming more and more principle-centered and less and less method focused. Methods are simply the tools to accomplish our principles. The beauty of being principle-centered is that you may accomplish a principle a certain way and it energizes and works for you. It may not work as well for someone else in the same way. The fact is, just because it works for you does not mean the way you approach that principle or live it out is for everyone. As a leader, know what works for you and enable others to find what allows them to be the best they can be.

For example:

I believe in the principle of being a lifelong learner. For me that translates into intentionality and reflection being an important part of my life. Lifelong learning comes from reading, courses, conversations, life experiences and relationships. It is about bite-size input and then reflecting on what does this mean and what does this mean in my life. I weigh it against my values. If it fits, I embrace it and seek to drop it into conversations as another way of embedding it in my life and not just in my mind. If it is great and yet is not where I am, then I let it go. I watch my friends get really excited about a theme and my first reaction is, "Oh I want to learn more about that too." Yet this can often be a distraction to what I really need to focus on and embrace in my life.

Learn what it means to stay true to your principles and values and what it means to shift in your methodologies. You will find that, as a general rule, you will find spaces of agreement on principles with people and you will find your greatest disagreements will be around methods.

Stick to the important and learn to let go of the lesser important for the greater purpose. As Stephen Covey has said so well, "Keep the end in mind."

✦ Kaleidoscope Reflections

1. What do you need to pay attention to about who or what you recognize as being bigger than yourself?

2. What do you need to pay attention to about yourself and your role, about others in your life and their role in your life?

Pay attention in order to adapt for accomplishing what is most needful. Adaptability is a proactive way to address differences and manage potential conflict.

The Best of Curiosity, Collaboration and Negotiation

The small space where the three circles intersect is the space that will draw you together. It becomes the necessary focus to keep measuring and moving towards leadership development in order to have positive movement forward and to work through expected and unexpected conflicts. Finding this sweet spot takes continual curiosity, conscious collaboration and healthy negotiation. These are the people skills that require consistent focus and reflection before taking bold action.

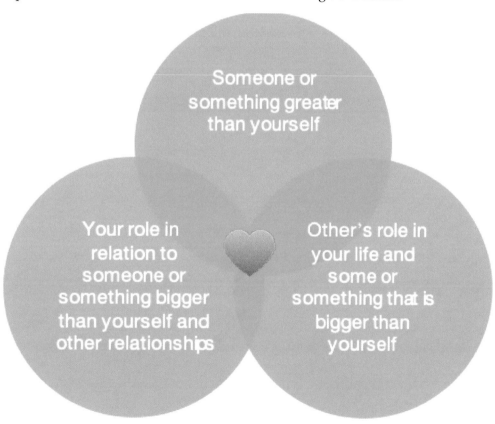

Notes—record your most significant thoughts to reflect on and to begin bold action.

_____

_____

_____

_____

_____

_____

_____

_____

_____

_____

_____

_____

_____

_____

_____

_____

_____

_____

_____

_____

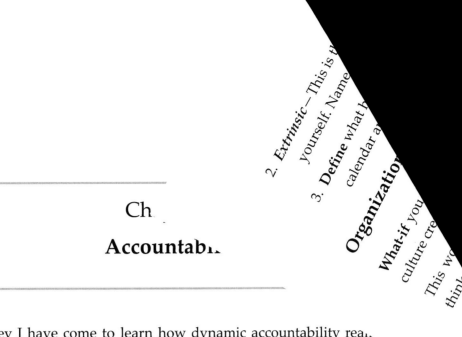

Ch...

Accountab...

In my leadership journey I have come to learn how dynamic accountability rea...

realize that I cannot hold anyone accountable for what I think they should do. I can o...

accountable for what they have told me they want to be accountable for. Accountability is a t...

street and is only as strong as the relational authenticity and trust that has been built in th...

relationship. Empowerment is a healthy component that works together with accountability, to bring clarity to the themes we looked at in the quadrant Analyze, as well as expectations, roles, responsibilities and timelines. As we look at growing ourselves, take some time to define the parameters of empowerment for your own growth. Engage the people and processes that create accountability to get to who you want to be and what you want to do.

Early on in my leadership, a dear older mentor taught me to ask two questions of trusted people in my life.

1. What do you see to celebrate in my life or what do you see going well?

2. What do you want to caution me about?

I don't know about you, but I have not met a person yet who is eager and waiting to be criticized. These two questions provide a way for you to seek feedback in order to see what you do not see and then to make the kaleidoscope adjustment that may be needed. By being upfront in your asking, you create a healthy culture for healthy feedback. You also come with a heart prepared to receive and process without the need to be defensive. When you can hear the feedback given, you can do something about it.

 Kaleidoscope Reflections

Accountability has two faces.

1. *Intrinsic*—This is about your inner drive, values and desire to be all you can be. Name and define these.

e people, the things, the philosophies that affect you from outside
and define these.

ealthy accountability looks like for you and then how that will fit on your
d with whom.

al Accountability

were part of a culture of accountability that was filled with abundance thinking and the
ted space for grace, clear expectations and outcomes?

uld apply to yourself first of all and then be nurtured throughout the organization. As you
of the accountability systems you have and why they are important in your organization, reflect
his quote and complete it from your experience. What word would you place in the blank space?

Engagement without accountability creates_____

Where does accountability fit in the organization or team you lead? Your leadership role has certain expectations and desired outcomes that you are to focus on; these should be stated clearly and have accountability in place. By the very nature of being called a leader, your role also comes with certain unspoken expectations. These may often be a challenge in an organization that is focused on tasks and ends primarily. Many of the unspoken, less defined and unclear expectations are often around working with and through people.

Your leadership role requires strong and accountable leadership in the following four areas:

1. A Culture Creator

The cultures that staff and volunteers thrive in best are cultures where the leadership has led the staff through a process of defining what the values of the organization are, based on the vision and mission of the organization. If the organization is new, primary focus one is to state and define what the vision and mission are, along with clarifying the values. As you do the work to define the vision and mission, discipline yourself to ask, "Why does that matter?" This will help to clarify your values.

As a leader in a few organizations both hired and as a volunteer, I made some observations which have influenced the following perspective on developing organizational vision, mission and values and also on leading with them in mind.

In one organization I was a part of, we worked hard to define with our team what the vision, mission and values were. We grappled hard to determine the words, the meanings and the outcomes. There was camaraderie, heated discussions, agreements and disagreements. There were times of wanting to quit or at least pull out one's hair or the leader's hair! What happened at the end of that process was full ownership for the living out what this hard-fought battle produced. We had skin in the game and so we owned it. My observation over time was that those who came to be a part of the organization, who had not battled to define who we were as an organization and what we were about, had very little ownership and often very little knowledge of our focus. They came into the organization for the job and brought their own perspectives, which often created tension and even pain (think back to the "Where We Get Stuck" model). A learning from this was how important it is to have an orientation that causes new hires to think about and own the organization's directional statements. This is crucial in leading with positive energy going forward.

In **Section 2**, you took an in-depth look at yourself through the strategic thinking model. That same model can be used for this organizational work as well.

 Kaleidoscope Reflections

1. How would you describe your present work culture? How would you describe what the organizational behaviours say is important?

2. Where do you see alignment?

3. Where do you see misalignment?

4. Describe what you understand about the organization's guiding principles and how you are living them out?

5. What are your observations about your gaps and your strengths in embracing these guiding principles and passing them on?

2. A Framework Manager

A framework is a basic structure providing support for a system, a concept, or a context. It provides the bare skeleton within which the organization can be built. Every organization has a variety of frameworks: an authority framework, a financial framework, a decision framework, a people framework, etc. A framework is mainly about things and so requires management. There is a level of clarity in the stated framework that allows for healthy accountability.

Leadership requires a definition and an accountability for effectiveness and meaning. If an organization is new, creating healthy frameworks is done with relative ease. If the organization is older, existing frameworks often are the stability that people cling to and will resist if there is any focus on changing them. A change like this creates discomfort and grief that brings on resistance. One way to help people move forward is to celebrate all they have done to get the organization to this point and to view it as the foundation that is being built on. Although the framework is to be managed, the people within the framework are to be led. As you create your people framework, be mindful that your role is to lead people not to manage them.

 Kaleidoscope Reflections

1. Take a moment to define and clarify each framework you are responsible to manage and to lead in your organization.

2. Reflect on where these frameworks are healthy and strong and where either some work to strengthen them is needed, or a new dream for them is needed.

3. A People Influencer

People are the heart of the organization. As you work with people the need increases to know yourself in order to appreciate and know your people.

> Ruth was very self-aware of her limitations and, in turn, hired those who shared similar values to her, but had different giftings. She loved to inspire her staff and leaders, and she led in a way that was freeing and empowering. She gave the overall vision for the direction she wanted us to go and then gave us permission to make suggestions for methods and processes about how to get there.
>
> Ruth's days were filled with people connections, which I would schedule for her. We established a rhythm where we would connect for the last fifteen minutes of each day (and yes, I put that in her calendar)! She would debrief from the meetings she had and forward to me any follow-up items that needed to be done and I would update her on her schedule for the following day. That became a very productive time for both of us.
>
> A colleague and I often joked that Ruth was the visionary—her head was often in the clouds dreaming of what could happen and where we could go . . . and we were on the ground holding onto her feet to try to keep her grounded! In keeping with that image, she never resisted that grounding—as long as she could keep moving forward in her ideation.
>
> My strengths are in the areas of achiever and responsibility, so making lists and crossing things off as they were completed was how I evaluated my productiveness. Ruth would propose an idea or project and then I would make a list of the steps necessary to achieve that (or, at times, share the list of reasons why it couldn't happen). Ruth trusted her staff and instead of micromanaging each step of the way, she freed us to accomplish our tasks.
>
> Ruth's goal was and is to create leaders and by enabling those around her to work within their areas of giftedness, she does that well.
>
> Vidette Heller, Executive Assistant

Components of Developing Influence:

• Discovering each other's strengths and how to create a collaborative culture is your role.

• Understanding each other's weakness in order to create a collaborative culture rather than competitive culture is vital for health and accomplishing desired outcomes.

• Developing strong listening skills serves to enable you as the leader to understand from more than one perspective. Three levels of listening produce different results.

Level 1—is about me, listening in order to talk is merely an exchange of words which may soon be forgotten. I am listening to you while relating what you are saying to my story. It becomes about me.

Level 2—is about you, listening and processing in order to reflect back and be sure you understand what is really being said. It becomes about you.

Level 3—is about everything seen and unseen that is influencing the conversation. Curious questions that are full of wonderment rather than judgment reveal more information for greater understanding and mutual perspective. It becomes about you, me and greater understanding.

In order to influence people, Level 3 listening is required. Then the environment is ready for true, informed communication that can draw people into what is needed next.

A note on curious questions. I was raised in an era where the culture said that children were to be seen and not heard. I am so grateful that my home, growing up, was counterculture and I was one curious child! And yet that culture affected the way I entered leadership. My beginning days of leadership were also in a culture that leaders were authoritative and dictatorial. The result: I never asked questions. What I did do was go away and think about it and often become judgmental. Although I was told to ask questions, because I had entered with a judgmental mindset, my questions came out sounding judgmental which shut down any communication very quickly. This did not serve me well, it meant I was not heard. I worked hard to understand, to learn and to find a better way. I researched and learned what it meant to be curious; to be full of wonder like a child with no judgmental load behind, just simple curiosity.

 Kaleidoscope Reflections

1. Reflect on what it would take for you to listen at Level 3.

2. What shifts do you need to make in your conversations?

3. Practice in your next few conversations just listening and asking curious, unloaded questions.

4. Reflect on what changed for you in this approach.

4. A Results Accountant

To create an abundant, accountable and productive organizational culture, the foundation is about paying attention to who and what you say you are and who and what you actually are.

Susan Scott, in her book *Fierce Conversations*, refers to this as official truth and ground truth. Do the people who work for you experience the same thing between what you say and the things you do? How would you describe the gaps between those two?

In Section 1 we referred to the story of the "Emperor Has No Clothes" as a clear picture of what that gap can look like to others and the gap in what we might miss ourselves. Keep the expectations and values clear and the accounting simple. Clarity around the expectations and values allows for an uncomplicated way to handle when differences arise. See section 2.

 Kaleidoscope Reflections

1. On a Balcony Day take the time to go through what the expectations and values are for yourself.

2. How would you describe what this is looking like in your leadership?

3. Name your direct reports, go through their role descriptions and your expressed expectations and values for them.

4. Reflect on the level of congruity you see and what needs to be clarified and communicated.

Accountability Process

Evaluation is progressive in each step and compiled at year end or performance review time. Your first responsibility is to your own accountability systems and processes. Any of these tools can be used at any time to address accountability for yourself and for your organization. It clarifies your need for intentional change as well as inadequate or inappropriate work.

The following are suggested tools that are important to develop, or sample tools that can be used or morphed to be applicable to you and the organization you lead.

• Vision, Mission, Values

Use the Strategic Thinking Model at the beginning of the section on Integration to flesh out your:

Vision—THERE—where you are going
Mission—How you will accomplish your vision
Values—How you will work together, what your decisions will be based on and why that is important

• Role and Responsibilities

This tool is vital to clear expectations and healthy accountability. This states the boundaries and freedoms found in empowerment and accountability.

The Empowerment/Accountability Matrix is built on the clarity of the Roles and Responsibilities document you create. Each employee's roles and responsibilities will be unique to the role they are hired to fulfill. One size does not fit all and yet a template can guide the creation of this document.

● Empowerment/Accountability Matrix

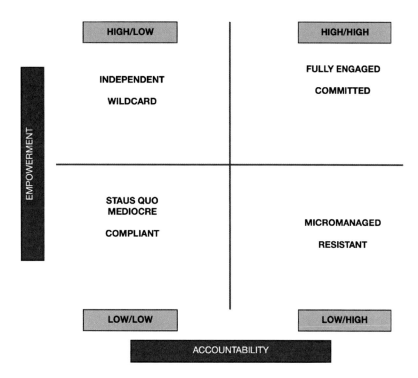

This matrix appears here for you to consider your leadership within its framework and then later in Section 3 – Transformation, when you consider your organizational culture framework.

What-if you showed up committed and were part of creating a fully engaged environment?

 Kaleidoscope Reflections

1. Take each quadrant and give a description from your perspective what a person's thoughts, attitudes and behaviours might be.

   1. Thoughts?
   2. Attitudes?
   3. Behaviours?

2. Put a check mark beside each one of those descriptors that describes you right now.

3. What quadrant is most typical of you right now and why do you think that is?

4. What quadrant would you like to be in?

5. Describe what it would take to move into that quadrant.

6. Who do you need to walk with you in this move?

7. What resources do you need to make this move? For example, where do you spend your time, how do you prioritize your life, etc.?

• Productivity/Attitude Matrix

This matrix also appears here for you to look at your leadership through this framework and then in Section 3—Transformation to consider your organizational culture through this framework.

What-if you were part of creating and leading a staff environment where each staff and volunteer knew what productivity and great attitude looked like as they worked to accomplish the ends of the organization in the role they were hired for or placed in?

Although productivity is easier and less messy to measure than attitude, attitude is often the fine line of success or failure for any employee, including leaders. The following matrix is useful for your leadership and also for those you lead and are responsible to coach or supervise.

Creating a Culture of Productivity and Great Attitudes

HIGH/LOW	HIGH/HIGH
Great Productivity Poor Attitude	Great Productivity Great Attitude
Poor Productivity Poor Attitude	Poor Productivity Great Attitude
LOW/LOW	LOW/HIGH

PRODUCTIVITY

ATTITUDE

 Kaleidoscope Reflections

Complete this matrix for yourself based on your roles and responsibilities and then you can use this as an engaging team development exercise.

1. Give clear, simple definitions for productivity and attitude, which are outside the matrix,

and then give clarifying and measurable definitions for the nuances found in each of the quadrants. These definitions within the quadrants can be made specific in relation to each person's roles and responsibilities.

2. Describe where you see yourself having the ability to succeed readily.

3. Describe where it will take more effort for you to succeed.

4. How would you describe the training or professional development it would take to increase your leadership capacity, or to increase each employee's capacity to meet the ends?

● Commitment—Code of How We Work Together

Every working group or team needs to work through a commitment and values document which will reflect how the team will choose to work together to achieve the ends that the organization requires. This document changes the conversations when issues arise. Creating the document together provides ownership on a deeper level than when employees are just handed a document to sign to signify their agreement. Once the document is created and new hires come on, this becomes a part of staff orientation and volunteer orientation.

Create a conversation around what is important for us all to agree on and what that could look like. When issues arise so do emotions. Refer back to the downward spiral in Section 1. The clash of expectations and current reality arise when there is a lack of clarity around vision, mission, values, roles and responsibilities. The commitment and values document helps to flesh out what often are unspoken family rules in an organization.

When an issue arises:

1. Acknowledge the emotion—how is each person feeling? Provide a space for them to explore and express why this is important to them. Recognize that high emotion often means one's values have been stepped on.

2. Acknowledge the gap between expectations and current reality. This means each person brings their perspective to the table to be worked with and to work towards the sweet spot where values draw together.

3. Acknowledge a commitment to listen to each other and to work within relational guidelines, which will focus on the issue, not the personality difference.

4. When it is all out on the table, guide the conversation based on the agreement around commitments and values to a common focus and how the differences can be mitigated and/or let go of as each situation demands.

● One to One Coaching

Executive and Leadership Coaching has a simple framework for helping people move forward in their roles and responsibilities. Coaching is about addressing present concerns for future benefit. It is client driven and coach supported.

1. The client brings their agenda to the conversation.
2. The client and coach explore that agenda for understanding and for all the possibilities surrounding the agenda.
3. When the client's energy spikes in the conversation, it is one clue that a potential answer has appeared and should be followed.
4. A plan is put in place with appropriate accountability for the client to know they are supported and will be followed through with.

This is a very simple framework that is easy to remember and can be enhanced as needed. There are some excellent coaching models, books and courses available. To read this framework and consider yourself a coach would not be true. Coaching is an art and requires great skill to use in a way that benefits the client. One of the hardest skills to develop is to learn to listen at the highest level, which means the coach is self-aware and is also aware of the client, the environment and how all that is happening is affecting the client and their processing to a meaningful plan. In my early days of coach's training, my instructor made the comment to our class, "If you think you have the right answer for the client, when you are highly energized and can't wait to speak, then you no longer have the client's best interests in mind."

 Kaleidoscope Reflections

1. As you consider that last comment in the last paragraph, what does it stir within you? Is there anything you need to do with this response?

2. What part of your thinking is ego driven and what part is client driven? What do you need to shift in your coaching conversations?

3. If you have not taken any coach's training, take the time to explore what leadership level coach's training would increase your leadership influence.

Notes—record your most significant thoughts to reflect on and to begin bold action.

Chapter 14

Final Thoughts on The Self-Leadership Growth Path

I can only imagine all that has been stirred within you as you have worked though these questions. These times of reflection are what keep us in touch.

As Frederick Buechner said, *"The place God calls you to is the place where your deep gladness and the world's deep hunger meet."*

If you have not done this type of reflection before, then this becomes a baseline as you continue to grow and develop in your leadership influence. You will discover a fresh awareness of your gladness space, of your regard for others, of a clear focus and ability to act with clarity and conviction. You will continually move towards greater integration and effectiveness. As you walk deeper into this ever learning and growing space, you will find your heart turning to move beyond your effectiveness to want to pour your life into others in a way that will enable them to live out where their deep gladness and the world's deep hunger meet. This is our journey; this is your calling.

Kaleidoscope Reflections

1. In light of all you have discovered in this exercise, how would you describe what makes your heart sing?

2. What need in the world causes you to sit up and take notice? When you watch the news, what makes you feel angry?

3. What brings you great joy?

4. Create as short a phrase as possible to describe this. This is your leadership mission statement. This is your message to the world. This is your passion. This gives you deep gladness. This fuels you in the daily duty and inspires you to keep going.

5. Create questions around this phrase that will hold you accountable to intentionally living this out loud all the time.

6. Consider who you need on this journey, to encourage you and to pour your life into. As you continue to age, who are the mentors you are sitting with in the decades younger than you? Seek them out. Learn from them. They are the future.

Kaleidoscope Reflections

Keeping a Mission Statement, Vision Statement, Life Purpose Statement, or Values Dynamic Alive

Now that you have gone to all the hard work of creating a statement to guide and direct you, it can become dynamic in your life as you use it to craft your decisions both large and small. Begin by creating a statement succinct enough and powerful enough that it comes to the tip of your tongue easily. Begin by using it each day as you set your plan for the day and then as you review your day. Making time for both these activities is crucial to living a purposeful and meaningful life. Soon this phrase will become like a second nature in your thought processes. Use it in conversation with your mentor to determine what they would celebrate about you in fully living this out and what would they caution you on where you might be missing the mark.

What-if this became alive and dynamic in your life and leadership?

This then would become what guides your thoughts and decisions. Consider how your life would become richer, fuller, more focused and fulfilling.

May you find your hearts and minds full and inspired as you face each day and each part of your self-leadership journey. May you find it to be a source of inspiration to pour into others in a way that brings them fulfillment and satisfaction in their roles of life.

As you come to a close of this section of Self-Leadership Development, here is your invitation to face the challenge of moving beyond delegation to investing in, entrusting to and empowering great leaders for the future. As we begin to shift our focus from who we are becoming to how we work with others, we will find such fulfillment as we see them become more strategic in their thinking, problem solvers and solution based. All the exercises you have completed in Section 1 and 2 can be applied as you invest and entrust to others.

What-if your investment was in those who are ready and capable of the challenge to rise above mediocrity, become strategic in their thinking and their leadership?

Notes—record your most significant thoughts to reflect on and to begin bold action.

Section III *Transformation*

Chapter 15
Introduction

"Transformation is a marked change in form, nature, or appearance." —Oxford Dictionary

What-if as leaders we were meant to grow, to morph, to change and by doing that to reproduce into the lives of others?

In the world of the butterfly, transformation is a dramatic picture of what we as leaders long for. Whatever there is in us that has been functional, and yet perhaps less than attractive, can be changed into a form that catches the attention of others. It invites them to follow us and will often do a gentle landing on us that affirms we are safe, approachable, credible and of worth. The butterfly paints the picture that we are all becomers on the journey and we have choice in becoming all we were put on this earth to accomplish.

Nature is filled with many examples of lifecycles that are normative and healthy. Each has a beginning, an ending and a new beginning. As transformative leaders, we are the keepers and influencers of that lifecycle in our spheres of influence. There will be times when we are called to dream, to build the dream, to fight for the dream, to nurse the dream, and at times to help the dream die with dignity. Then other dreams can arise and move us forward in strategic, intentional and formative ways.

A number of years ago I began a journey in a contract position with an organization that was focused on growing more confident and competent leaders. Although I had led for many years with many similar strategies, that first year was like being thrown into the deep end of the pool and given the opportunity to sink or swim. It was invigorating, terrifying and compelling.

Several years later one of the founders and myself saw the need for a change in order to create a space for the organization to be the most effective it could be in the market we now faced. There was no business to sell and yet there was an incredibly effective concept to pass on that would continue to influence and deepen the leadership of the nonprofit sector. The baton was passed to an organization of choice and so began the transition of a concept whose essence was powerful and effective.

Transitions are a time to reaffirm the essence and hold everything else with open hands. Our founder used the analogy of holding a bird in our hand. The analogy is to hold the bird firm enough so that it does not fly away and yet loose enough that it doesn't crap on your hand or die! This is the concept of tensions, tensions that we all face constantly.

Now my role was to navigate those tensions well for transitioning the essence and letting go of the inessential. In so doing we allowed for something better or stronger, for increasing our effectiveness for today. In a three year time period of transition into the new organization there were intriguing challenges such as:

- major senior staff turnover four times in three years
- conflicting values
- personality conflicts
- times of distrust, lack of clarity, lack of communication, and many assumptions
- the program was organic, the new environment it was moving into was corporate

I moved from an apprentice in a leadership development program, to transitioning that very effective leadership program into a larger organization. There were inherent challenges and so many incredible learnings along the way. Transformation was not just about me, it was about freeing others to be transformed and even for this highly effective program to be freed to be transformed.

I have worked with organizations that have had years of incredible success by the dream of a founder. I have also watched when the founder lost focus on the principles that had made the organization so successful and became focused on the methods (the way we have always done this) to fulfill those principles.

Transitions are a very hands-on time for affirming what stops transformation and what makes it move forward either with a surge or with a slow and steady pace. It affirms the need for leading through the natural laws of life, death and rebirth. These laws are the same. As Stephen Covey describes it, *it is the law of the land*. The natural way of our world works in the progression of birth, new growth, maturation, degeneration and an opportunity for rebirth. Rebirth comes from what has died or been let go of and what has become nonessential or ineffective. Without an intentional focus on paying attention to this cycle, we can get lost in what we invested in and feel slighted when improvements or changes are suggested.

The Law of Nature

There are laws of nature that are intrinsic to life and death. They are set and even as we seek to influence them, they remain. As we consider the rhythms of leadership and the organizations we lead, they are so similar. By paying attention, we can influence the length of the health and longevity of ourselves as leaders and of the organizations we lead.

In organizations we see:

• BIRTH—a great idea appears! This may be a very short time frame, or it may percolate for a while as different approaches are tried. The question: What will it take to nurture and help this idea to get established?

• NEW GROWTH—evidence of this new life is seen. The question: What will ensure that growth is ongoing and does not stagnate?

• MATURATION—the great idea begins to mature and take on a shape that is effective. This can go on for years and rich outcomes are realized. It also can come to a stuck spot that requires the organization to rethink. The question: What needs to be added to keep the idea engaging and inspiring for all?

• DEGENERATION—the mature idea begins to get ragged around the edges and needs some tweaking. This season can last for any amount of time. The question: What has happened that is creating a breakdown and what is your part in either seeing it restored, or in helping it end with dignity so something new can be born?

• DEATH—the mature idea can begin to die on its own, or as leadership pays attention, they have the opportunity to help the idea die with dignity while beginning to embrace newness. The question: What does respect, and celebration look like in order to let go and move on?

• REBIRTH—this is the cycle of newness taking shape and moving to new growth and maturing again. The question: What are the necessities for this life to prosper?

This is an ever-repeating cycle. It is a cycle that as leaders we see in our own leadership and in our own spheres of influence. There is an innate part of our human nature that knows all things being equal success takes hard work. Yet we also think that all the hard work we do should result in outcomes as we have planned them to be. We often are taken aback by our hard and good work not always resulting in the results we had planned. It reminds me again of the concept introduced earlier that leadership success is like holding a bird in our hands. We need to hold it tight enough to keep it safe and loose enough it does not die.

Kaleidoscope Reflections

1. As you consider the never-ending cycle above, where would you place yourself as a leader in that cycle?

2. What reflections and bold action does that space require of you?

3. What would it look like to be excellent at whatever stage you find yourself?

4. Where would you place your organization within that cycle?

5. What reflection and bold action will it take to be healthy, effective and strong as possible?

Notes—record your most significant thoughts to reflect on and to begin bold action.

Chapter 16
Lifelong Leadership Learning

What-if leaders were lifelong learners who understood the power of leadership development for themselves and for growing leaders for the future?

As we begin this section, we move from Inspiration—navigating the realities of our own leadership development, Integration—navigating our integration as a leader, to Transformation—navigating the long game of investing in others.

I often refer to this as "The Cookie Principle."

As a mom with young children and having health issues that would often side-track me, I came to realize I needed to learn the "cookie principle." When I was well, I loved to cook and bake. It was one way I loved on my family. One time when I was not well and lying in bed, I realized how much there was to be done. I was not able to pull my part of the load. I came to an aha moment. I could continue to be the one who shared her love through doing all the baking, or I could share my love by teaching my children to bake. The first way would only ensure cookies in the lunch bags when I was well enough to do the baking. The investment of teaching my kids to bake meant that no matter what my health status, they would and could have cookies all the time. It meant investing time to teach, to allow for success and for failure, to let go, to celebrate and to move forward. This simple little aha has been there for me all through my leadership days as well. I could be the one to do it all, or I could do what it takes to entrust others and empower them for so much more than I could do alone. As a leader I could be the one to be the fixer who everyone runs to, or I can become the enabler of good strategic thinking in my employees and volunteers.

This **What-if** question above arose early for me in my leadership days both in retail management, in church ministry and as a contractor. I found so many incredible people who are employees spending the bulk of their waking hours in a position or role that was so much more than the daily task roster. These were the eager learners and the ones who wanted to become so much more. My father used to say, "You can lead a horse to water, but you can't make him drink." Then he would pause and say, "But you can throw salt in the oats and make him thirsty!" Figuratively speaking, I loved to throw salt in the oats of these potential leaders and watch their thirst to learn and develop increase.

As I was entrusted with leadership roles, I came to the realization that I had been given so many great opportunities to develop over my lifetime and not everyone was given those kinds of opportunities. It was so easy to think about creating a one size fits all and yet I had also experienced what it was like to be treated like a widget. This often ignored what I brought to my role. It was focused on treating everyone the same in spite of their uniqueness. It was about the fairness quotient of professional development dollars over the investment power of those same dollars. It expected that if everyone received the same training, it would produce stellar results and stellar employees of all. Unfortunately, it did not accomplish that. I began to research, to experiment with so much of what was intuitive to me. My mission statement should have been Nike's "Just Do It!" And yet for me, it was a gradual and then sudden dawning that we were all created uniquely, and our life experiences taught us differently. This meant that principle based professional development allowed for purpose, structure and individualization. When the professional development size fit the individual, the people grew exponentially, and the organization increased.

Two processes that come into play in lifelong learning.

1. Developing yourself as a leader
2. Transformative leadership development

Notes—record your most significant thoughts to reflect on and to begin bold action.

Chapter 17

Developing Yourself As A Leader

What-if each person is worthy of being seen as an individual and given opportunity to be developed in a way that gives them space to be the best they can be?

If you completed your leadership lifeline back in Section 2 under **Analyze,** you will have discovered some of the varied ways that had a significant impact on who you are and how you lead today. You also may have come to understand that in each situation that developed, you brought a uniqueness to it that fit you and the season of leadership you were in. It was where the rubber met the road for you and so you were changed.

Over the years, I have been intrigued by the finances that organizations spend to grow leaders. I have also been intrigued by the lack of thought given to the effectiveness of methods and the power of healthy accountability within organizations. As we look at some universal principles around leadership development, you will have aha moments of what is working in your leadership influence. You will be challenged for what you also could be doing for greater effectiveness.

Early in my years of leadership, I was deeply influenced by Leroy Eims who maintained that people needed different methods for growth and life change. He maintained that developing people had a bell curve. There were leaders who were focused on learning and growth and ready to go at a faster pace when it came to embracing and applying their learnings. There were those that were more methodical and perhaps appeared slower, who also were focused on embracing and applying their learnings. These two groups benefitted from more individual coaching than group teaching and learning. There were also the bulk of leaders who benefit from the large-scale growth opportunities. Often the missing piece for making these large-scale learning opportunities effective is accountability for application of the learnings.

As leaders we have been told over and over that leaders are readers and it is true. And yet leaders are so much more than readers. Leaders are learners who find learnings through and in any situation and/or relationship they are a part of. These learnings shape them, change them and produce character, competence and confidence.

The **Leadership Development Impact Model** was created in order to hold healthy discussions on the effectiveness of our outlay of finances, the time and learning themes in the life of the individual employee and a healthier bottom line for the organization. All learning opportunities and methods have a purpose and a place. The most common forms of professional development are the focus of the Leadership Development Impact Model. Each has a significant place in professional development and some by nature have a greater effect on transformative leadership than others. Over the years I observed that no matter where I served in the organization, generally speaking those who thrive and are thirsty, and those who struggle and are thirsty, will benefit the most from the lower spectrum on the triangle below.

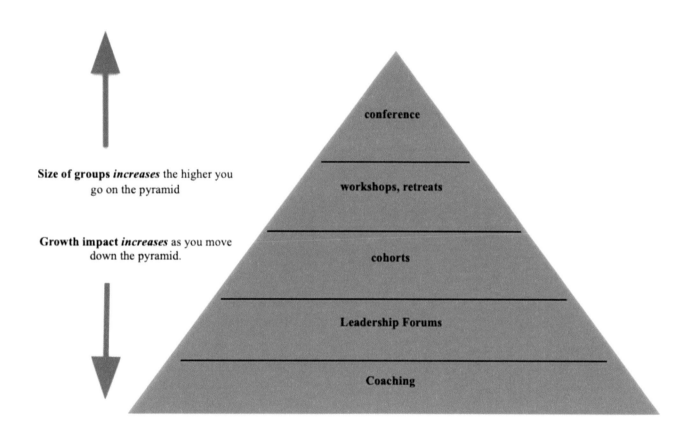

What-if the essence of leadership development was about growth and accountability that changes you and those you lead?

The **Leadership Development Impact Model** focuses on the effectiveness of each format for learning and who benefits most from each format.

1. **Conferences,** generally speaking, have the largest number of attendees and the least impact on actual leadership development in the long term. We all can think of the snippets and often powerful snippets that we walked away from conferences with. They often held aha moments that as we sit with no responsibilities except to listen, our minds grasp something in a new or different way that makes sense like it never has before. Conferences provide a wealth of information and knowledge and yet provide very little time for meaningful reflection,

internalizing and planning for bold action and/or life change. Skill focused conferences benefit professions such as health care, education, etc.

It is the role and responsibility of the sending organization to decide what they want to see accomplished through this form of professional development. Their responsibility will be to create healthy accountability systems in order to encourage life-changing learning for the individual. It will also encourage the growth and increasing maturity of the organization.

2. **Workshops, Retreats** vary in size. Knowledge is more focused. Opportunity for conversation and/or discussion is often available. It gives food for thought and broader perspectives. Growth and transformative change is dependent on size, focus and desired outcomes that the planner has put into place. Relationship and reflection can add to the growth potential of a retreat or workshop.

3. **Cohorts** are composed of 10–20 participants with a common bond (ex. All executive directors, emerging leaders, all men, all women, etc.). This will allow for maximum processing of focused themes towards leadership life change in a safe, relational setting. Peer learning and accountability is a natural byproduct of the trust invested in the cohort relationships.

4. **Leadership Forums** are generally 4–8 participants who sign on because of the theme and bring their perspective and research for greater enriching and practical leadership life change. Group accountability is built into the culture.

5. **One to One Coaching** provides for maximum leadership life change impact for those on either end of the bell curve of learning. The client brings their agenda to be explored and to be defined as to what would be the most effective takeaway and then held accountable for the bold action they choose to commit to.

Believing that a one size fits all in professional development is a myth that will not produce strong, responsible leaders. Facilitating professional development is based on good stewardship of time, talent and treasure entrusted to you for personal, professional growth, accountability and healthy change. It is rarely clean and tidy and yet it yields effective opportunities for life and leadership growth.

 Kaleidoscope Reflections

As leaders, a good starting point is to use a tool like the *Self-Leadership Growth Path* in Section 2 - **Integration**. Ask each person to complete this tool, giving them a reasonable timeline. Combine this with the vision, values and mission of the organization and the role the leader was hired to fulfill. This tool along with one-on-one coaching will produce leaders who are future focused, present minded and ready to move forward.

An equation for professional development success: Purpose statement and values of the leader + the role they were hired to fulfill + vision, mission and values of organization = a direction for personal and professional development that benefits the leader and the organization.

The *Self-Leadership Growth Path* will reveal what and how each staff member could have the greatest and most effective development both personally and professionally. The end result will also reveal who the willing are and how to work with them. It will show you how to lead the less than willing to embrace opportunities for growth or help them move on to a better fit. Every staff person should have a clear role description. It includes clarity around expectations and accountability processes. This will allow them to be accountable to the desired outcomes that are in line with the mission and vision of the organization. Throughout this process the aim is to keep people current in their understanding of what the current reality is which is excellent preparation for heading into change that ultimately comes. This kind of staffing culture decreases complaining, gossip and discontent and keeps employees engaged in what is the most important, forward focused and aligned as a team. The focus shifts from maintaining programs to developing people, which is *Transformative Leadership Development*.

Notes—record your most significant thoughts to reflect on and to begin bold action.

Chapter 18
Transformative Leadership Development

Whatever the leadership role we fulfill, developing others for the present and the future is imperative. So many times I have watched leaders thrown into higher levels of leadership with the expectation that they will know how to move from task orientation to leading people. We often create the drama that drives us crazy. We rescue when we should be investing in and giving opportunity to make mistakes, learn, get up, try again and become the leaders for tomorrow.

Process for Transformative Leadership Development

What-if every leader had an intentional plan to develop the leaders they hired to become all they could be?

Following is a process that produces resilient, persevering, trustworthy leaders with a mindset to invest and entrust to others:

1. Create a Strategic Map for Transformative Leadership Development

Inspire, Analyze, Acquire, Act—The Self Leadership Path from Section 2 - Integration is a tool that can be used and applied to your process for developing the candidate in front of you.

2. Identify Potentials

Develop clear criteria, role descriptions and expectations as you seek to identify potential leaders. Move beyond looking for the ready-made; pay attention to the diamond in the rough. Skills can be taught and by nature learned. Character and attitude come from within the person and are the foundation for healthy leaders. Develop a set of character revealing questions that will show you the character and attitude of the candidate.

3. Invite Potentials

Create a relational and clear process to invite potential leaders to take the next step in their development and service. What would be important for you to pay attention to that is aligned with the organization, its vision, mission and values?

4. Assess

Strength Finder, Stand Out, Kolby, Enneagram, 360 Refined (EQ and Leadership), Belbin Star, Splash, DISC, Grip Birkman, Ministry Match etc. Any assessments that are useful to identify strengths, skills, personality, ways of being will enhance understanding for you as the leader and for the potential candidate and their development.

5. Individualize

Create an orientation that provides the most foundational information about the organization and its people. Create a next level expectation map. If they are to continue to move forward in their leadership, what do they need to be aware of, who do they need to have conversations with and even build relationships with, what skills will they need to develop to a greater degree and what is the accountability for their pursuit of this information?

Create an individualized development curve and timeline in relation to role expectations and organizational goals. These are prioritized by character (thoughts, attitude and behaviour) and skills (particular abilities for the role), both personally and professionally.

If this is a second level leadership role, what areas of the organization do they need to become more aware of? For example, if they became more aware of what the work of the board is about, in what ways would that enhance their leadership role?

What else might they need to start learning more about—for example finances? Social media?

6. Account

Define direct report expectations—what they must report on, to whom, by when, and why that matters (this is an opportunity to revisit the vision, mission, and values of the organization and the leader).

Develop an accountability plan, process and timeline.

Set expectations around organizational behaviour or work culture based on the organization's values. Also consider if the leader's values align with the organizational values. This creates great synergy, ownership and movement forward for all.

Keep short relational accounts.

7. Evaluate

This is done by outlining the clear expectations that have been identified and the timeline created. Evaluations can take different forms and have different purposes.

For example, here is an effective tool I used with my staff weekly. In implementing it there certainly were tensions around how it was originally being viewed. As relational leadership and expectations provided ongoing clarity, it was adopted without complaint. It is called the Four Q's and is to be used in a relational manner for it to work most effectively. Four Q's stand for four questions I asked my staff to give me at the end of their work week. The tool was created out of a sense of not being as in touch with a growing staff as I wanted to be. I was not a micro-manager. I simply wanted to know what was keeping my staff going and where there were things to address immediately, rather than allowing them to fester and grow out of proportion.

The Four Q'S

The Four Q's is a document I created to be used in a relational way as my staff grew. I wanted to stay in touch with how they were and with the challenges and celebrations they were experiencing in their role.

1. Ask and expect each member as a part of a normal work week to end their week by answering the four following questions or a variation of them.

- What did you accomplish this week?

    This was factual and also a place where I expected them to brag to me. I wanted to celebrate with them. For them the benefit was that it helped them wrap up their week and see what they actually had accomplished.

- What did you find challenging this week?

    I wanted to understand from their perspective what had been challenging and in a non-threatening way allow them to express this.

- What do you need from me?

  At times this would entail what I could do for them. At other times it allowed me to understand the kinds of resources they needed so that we could accomplish the outcomes we were working towards.

- What are you most grateful for?

  This is the spirit in which I wanted to approach my work and I wanted our work culture to evidence gratefulness rather than entitlement.

2. These were to be handed in by the end of their work week.

3. The leader's responsibility was to read them as soon as possible at the end of the week, which meant creating time in the calendar for this to happen.

4. As I used this tool, I read each direct report email through and I would pay attention to my gut responses to what I was reading. I used those gut responses to know whether I needed to give them a quick call, or a short visit to their desk to see if there was a need for an immediate discussion. Or, was it something they wanted to discuss next week, or at our monthly one-to-one meeting, or monthly team meeting?

5. I knew, and continued to learn, that timing is crucial in gaining and giving trust and for building a healthy team.

This tool is to be used in the context for building trusting relationships, not simply for a reporting of tasks. Over the course of the year we had other forms of evaluation: the organization's 360, the performance review, the one-to-one coaching sessions and the team meetings. An ongoing discovery was that where relationship was high, the greatest growth and leadership effectiveness developed.

I remember one staff person sharing with me that at first they felt this was a waste of time and they had better things to do. When their time came to move on from the role they fulfilled on our team, they spoke to how this tool became a welcome practice as it allowed them to wrap up their week and to leave work at work. They knew they did not have to go home carrying an emotional load over some unresolved issue. It would be talked about and right-sized before they headed home.

After I had moved onto another part of my career, I had one of my former staff come to me and say they have kept using the Four Q's because it has allowed them to have conversations before there were issues. This only works, of course, as trust is built with each other.

Over the years and relating to numerous employees, experience is a wonderful reminder that we can never assume another perspective. For many years I had carried a dream of starting a particular program. I knew I couldn't spread any thinner and so I put the dream on a back burner. A wonderful person, who caught that dream when I shared it with them, contacted me. I hired them in a contract position. I was eager to set them up for success and I loved their ability to get things done while relating well with people. Sometime into that year I began to notice resistance in certain areas.

This resistance was often revealed in the Four Q's. This gave me the opportunity to address the concerns as we went along. Near the end of the year-long contract, I knew that this resistance was not a good thing moving forward for either this employee or myself. I arranged to meet for a conversation around how they were feeling about the role, about me as their leader and about the future. As we talked it became evident and was shared openly by both of us that this was a contract that would be a one-year contract only. As the meeting came to a close, I wrote a summary of this meeting from my perspective and sent it to them. Recently going back to clean out files I came across many of the Four Q's this employee had filled out. I also came across the summary. This summary affirmed our mutual decision to complete the contract. This was another lesson in the wisdom of weighing perspectives, even when as a leader you might feel you are right. You learn there are other viewpoints to work with to bring everyone to that sweet spot of agreement.

On the following pages are additional evaluation resources.

Self—Assessment

Name:
Position:
Due Date:
Discussion Date:

The purpose of this document is to help you think through the perceptions that you hold of your job and the self-fulfillment you are finding in your work.

---

1. What achievements are you particularly proud of from this last year? What strengths have you shown?

---

2. What challenges or issues did you face a year ago and are they similar today? If so what does that mean?

---

3. What changes have there been in your role in the last year? What has that been like for you?

---

4. What changes have happened in your work environment that have caused you stress? How would you describe that stress?

5. What problems or challenges did you encounter in carrying out your role this last year? How did you overcome them? Are there still barriers to achieving job satisfaction? What are they?

Thank you for the time and effort you have taken to look at yourself and your job and expressing your perspective on both. Please feel free to add any other comments or questions.

1. Self-Assessment

In each organization where I have worked there have been official evaluations to be filled out for the Human Resources department. This brief little Self-Assessment has yielded more helpful information than any other evaluation I have used.

1. It is a way of hearing from each person what that person is proud of. As their leader, you may have been proud of any number of things about their performance or about themselves. This gives you an onside look at what was important to them. It also creates space for future conversations that align with what they are proud of and what the organization and you as their leader need to accomplish those.

2. You may think you know what challenged them and you may be right. This question allows a deeper look at how they express what challenged them and why that matters to them.

3. You now can understand what they considered changed, which you may have just considered everyday expectations.

4. This information ties in with question number 3, to give greater understanding about how they work and how work affects them.

5. This question gives insight into how much or how little they have grown. Are they facing the same challenges? Together you determine where the gap is and what each can do to mitigate those challenges.

2. Inner Leadership Evaluation

"A human being always acts, feels and performs in accordance with what they imagine to be true about them self and their environment."
Peter Urs Bender

Answer these questions: What do I believe to be true about myself?

Put a check mark by those words that describe what you believe about yourself.

competent	incompetent	patient
worthy	unworthy	impatient
victor	victim	willing to serve
gentle	aggressive	proud
optimistic	pessimistic	peaceful
passionate	blah!	anxious
risk taker	careful	
joyful	discouraged	

What do I believe about the organization I serve in? If I was asked to tell someone what it is, how would I describe it?

How was my perspective formed?

What do I need to take responsibility for?

1. My spiritual condition:

    How would I describe my spirituality and how do I feel about it? What indicators do I use to know the answer to that question?

    Is it by the things I do or who I am becoming?

2. How am I dealing with difficult people or situations? Is the purpose restoration or destruction?

    Do I use gasoline or water?

    Can I listen without being defensive?

    Do I understand when I must take a stand and when I need to leave it alone?

3. Is pride showing up in my life? (critical spirit, murmuring, complaining, ungratefulness)

    Do I recognize how pride shows up in my life? Name it. Name your plan to deal with it.

    Ask your superiors, your peers, your family, those who work with or for you. Do they see any evidences of pride in your life? If you can't ask, then you probably have a problem with pride!

4. Do you know yourself?

    List three of your greatest strengths:

    List three of your greatest weaknesses:

    List three of the easiest temptations you give into:

    List three of the greatest refreshers for you spiritually, emotionally and physically: Describe the kind of people you need to surround yourself with.

5. How am I dealing with inner disappointments, hurts, losses?

6. a. Do I see inner warning signals that I am not in good health emotionally, physically, spiritually, mentally? What are they?

    b. Do I allow myself the downtimes, even times of discouragement, after seasons of high giving or ministering? What do I need to do to free myself to move through this exercise?

7. Do I see myself developing and maturing in:

- Spirituality

- Character

- Skills and Abilities

- Wisdom

- Strategic thinking abilities

- People leadership and influence

- Conflict management—both intrinsic and extrinsic

Reflection and Bold Action needed:

8. Am I experiencing patterns with any of the following?

- Frustration

- Impatience

- Anger

- Lack of compassion

- Disdain

Reflection and Bold Action needed:

9. Who is responsible for this? What decision(s) are you avoiding? No decision is a decision to deal with the consequences.

Reflection and Bold Action needed:

10. Are there times I have difficulty being truthful with myself? What are the hindrances to be being truthful?

11. What three steps should I be taking in the next month to ensure the inner strength and health I need will either be maintained or restored?

3. The Healthy Staff Culture Pyramid

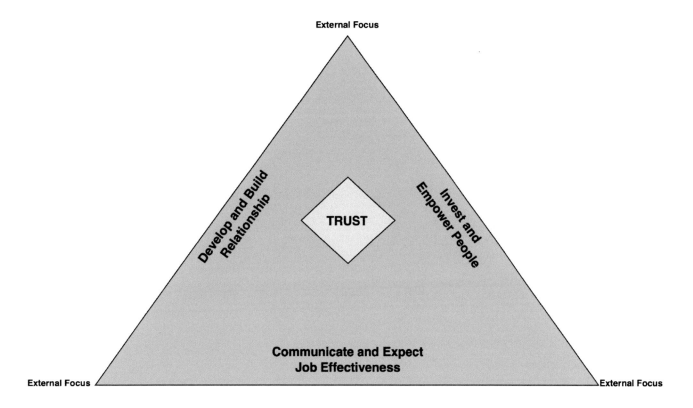

This diagram focuses on the mission over the organization, trust over control, client over entitlement. All that transpires within the culture creates space for an external client focus rather than an organization centric focus.

 Kaleidoscope Reflections

Use a simple sliding scale from 1–4 to determine where you need to be paying attention to in order to have a healthy staff culture. 1 rarely; 2 sometimes; 3 often; 4 typical.

1. Develop and build relationship—scale of 1–4

2. Investing in and empowering people—scale 1–4

3. Communicating and expecting job effectiveness—scale 1–4

4. Mission over organization—scale 1–4

5. Trust over control—scale 1–4

6. Client over entitlement—scale 1–4

What are your observations and what will be your plan?

Observations re Scores	Plan based on Observations

The Communication Template is for creating a process of clear communication with accountability built in. The template below reflects the decisions made and information needed. Templates serve to create a strategic approach, which can be passed on as process to new employees as with consistent use it becomes intuitive. Certain values are inherent to creating a healthy accountability where evaluation is welcome and seen as a part of moving closer to accomplishing the vision.

WHAT	WHY	WHO	WHEN	HOW
	Why it matters that this information is passed on	Name all the levels this information must pass through	What is the deadline for having this information passed on?	What methods of communication will be used to get this information out to the right people
Ex. extra $ is being made available for Professional Development this Budget Year. **All requests for PD must come through the (name your financial process team)**				

The transformative leadership values embraced are:

✓ Relational—using a strong relational foundation to influence the give and take of conversations

✓ Trustworthy—each person seeking to choose to behave in a way that increases trust amongst the team.

✓ Clear—learning the give and take of clarity in expectations. Clarity comes from heading into the tension of what I knew I meant and what others heard or experienced what I had said. As a leader investing in others, I often had to work the tension, especially when speed was great. I had to learn to stop and to ask if everything was clear. Much humble pie was consumed along the way!

✓ Creative—we were all to bring our best ideas to the table. That also created a tension when I as a leader was abounding with ideas!

It became a known fact that my team traveled under what they affectionately came to call the *cloud of unknowing*. A meaningful and memorable time for me was the day we celebrated together my leaving my senior leadership role. Part of the day was spent creating glass fused coffee coasters. Each one was to create a coaster that represented something that reminded them of me. At the end of that creative endeavour, they shared what they had made. My associate presented me with a coaster that had a large cloud in the upper left-hand corner, a sun in the upper right-hand corner, grass across the bottom, small coloured seeds in the grass on the lower left corner and blooming flowers on the far right lower corner. The meaning was that most of the time the team travelled under a cloud of unknowing, which eventually, they all agreed, got to the clarity the sun brought and the seeds grew into beautiful flowers. Recently my associate said to me, although there were often clouds of unknowing, as we all brought our abilities to the table, they became what the original vision was! Creativity at its best!

✓ Accountable—For me accountability is one of the most misunderstood and also disliked words in leadership. Often this is because it is nebulous and unclear. To say someone is accountable to you, and for you not to provide the explanation of what that means in the strength of relationship and context is ineffective, irresponsible and irritating at best.

 Kaleidoscope Reflections

If we want to have a leader investment culture, then we need to consider:

1. What must we keep to enable this to happen?
2. What must we celebrate and retire for this to happen?
3. What is the structure that will support this happening?
4. How will we manage the technical and adaptive changes that are needed? Name them.
5. Who will be responsible for what?
6. When will we make it possible?
7. Realistically, what is our willingness and capacity to enable this to move forward and to continue to grow and deepen?
8. What obstacles might we encounter? How will we mitigate these concerns and even risks?

Notes—record your most significant thoughts to reflect on and to begin bold action.

_____

_____

_____

_____

_____

_____

_____

_____

_____

_____

_____

_____

_____

_____

_____

_____

_____

_____

Chapter 19

Tensions in Leadership

What-if we recognized that our role as leaders was to navigate the tensions that face us each day?

"Our deepest fear is not that we are inadequate. Our deepest fear is that we are powerful beyond measure. It is our light, not our darkness, that most frightens us. We ask ourselves, "Who am I to be brilliant, gorgeous, talented, fabulous?" Actually, who are you not to be? You are a child of God. Your playing small does not serve the world. There is nothing enlightened about shrinking so that other people won't feel insecure around you. We are all meant to shine, as children do. We were born to make manifest the glory of God that is within us. It's not just in some of us; it's in everyone. And as we let our own light shine, we unconsciously give other people permission to do the same. As we are liberated from our own fear, our presence automatically liberates others."
by Marianne Williamson

The call to leadership and the role of leadership by its very nature creates a multitude of tensions for us to learn to navigate. All kinds of influences put pressure on the leader as they face multiple decisions that range from simple, to complicated, to complex.

In the book *Getting to Maybe* by Frances Westly, Brenda Zimmerman and Michael Quinn Paton, the authors give us a clear understanding of the difference between the following three factors: Simple is baking a cake by following a recipe. Complicated is sending a rocket to the moon by keeping rigid protocols and processes. Complex is like raising a child—need I say more?

Protocols, experience, processes, rules, recipes do not exist for one size fits all. And yet wisdom, principles, ability to think and discernment all play a role in moving forward. Technical challenges tend to be simple and usually can be resolved with an expert in that area and the manual at hand. Complicated challenges take a combination of clear processes, policies and protocols that will cover an array of technical and adaptive changes. Complex challenges will take people skills, intuitive and quick responses, authenticity, transparency and the ability to bring a sense of symmetry or unity from diversity similar to the twist of a kaleidoscope.

Kaleidoscope Reflections

1. Take a moment to think about a day of your choosing and list the tensions or the kinds of tensions you face.

2. How do you handle tension presently?

3. Where is tension getting the better of you?

4. What is one thing you can do to learn to navigate tension in a life-giving way?

Matrixes are great tools to recognize the kinds of tensions we face, and they give us ways to navigate and maximize on those differences. As you continue to read, you will discover matrixes that have been given prior thought and are filled in. You can take those same matrixes and start from a blank space, filling in the details to make it represent the language that reflects your culture and work ethic.

Tension in Leadership

Leadership in our time, no matter what field, provides opportunity, education, challenge, and tension. We are in a time where one of the certainties in leadership is that leaders need to navigate the winds of change. Ultimately the success of an organization depends on its ability to navigate change.

My experience deals with adjusting to a change in leadership in the midst of implementation of a change in culture from an inward and isolated atmosphere in the organization to a more inclusive, outward focus where the volunteer network was being encouraged to take a more active role. There was an intentionality to develop new leaders by having the current leaders responsible for various departments of the organization were really encouraged to recruit and train others to take over their responsibility, so they were able to look for opportunities to broaden and grow their own leadership experience.

The process was several years in development and was gaining some traction. The leadership structure had two layers -a governance leadership team and a team responsible for leading the day to day activity of the organization. The governance group tended to take a position where they were relying on the day to day team to develop programming and were, in general, reluctant leaders, functioning out of a sense of responsibility and not particularly capable of casting vision, modelling leadership, and demonstrating by example the qualities and characteristics they expected from others in the organization.

The greatest difficulties they struggled with were being able to make decisions, relying on their life and business experience and being able to disagree and work toward compromise or to negotiate a way forward that served the best interest of the organization. Frequently decisions were bogged down. Progress was slow in reaching consensus and providing day-to-day leadership with direction. I would suggest the handicap that created the unhealthy environment was "groupthink." My experience time and again would result in the circumstance that you could talk to the leaders individually and have them express themselves and then find out that when they met as a group their decision or outcome would be different and create confusion and frustration.

This environment became further complicated when one of the day to day leaders (the senior leader) left to accept another opportunity, leaving me as the leader in the second chair to carry on until a replacement could be found. Governance leadership at first assigned the outgoing senior leader to have primary responsibility for leading the transition team and only mid-course did they decide my role should be responsible to lead the transition.

The Governance leaders had primary responsibility and played a direct role in hiring the new senior leader.

The candidate they choose assumed his responsibility and did not have the same qualities as his predecessor. He had a more traditional view of the way things should be and reverted to a more inward and isolated path and had limited regard for the accomplishments that had been achieved over

the past years. There was little time allowed to become aware of the current environment and this resulted in tension among the day-to-day leadership team.

Outcome

The governance leaders were aware of the tension and did little to try and understand the dynamics of what was happening. Based on independent advice, the leaders reached a decision that the tension could not be mediated, and I was terminated without cause.

The result was not accurately communicated to the organization, resulting in program disruption and a number leaving the organization. The responsibilities, which were partly mine, were not reassigned and the momentum that had been gained after several years of effort suffered a setback.

Lesson Learned

Leadership is challenging at all levels. Leading from a position of confidence, with a large measure of humility and the conviction that you want to be a leader is critical. Important skills required of leadership include strength in communication, conflict resolution and a large measure of relational skills.

In building team, you need a good cross section of skills on the team. Each position needs to have clear definition and you want to avail yourself of and rely on the strengths of your team in order to best function and achieve optimum results.

Jack Ashby

1. Empowerment and Accountability Matrix

What-if our work culture was a healthy mix of empowerment and accountability?

In the following matrix, the first word in each box represents the culture of the organization; the second word describes the employee outlook.

In creating an environment for team growth and development, consider what each quadrant is about and use this tool to assess where you are as an empowered and accountable team.

Quadrant 1 The environment is *independent*; the person is a *wildcard*. Quadrant 2 The environment is *fully engaged*; the person is *committed*. Quadrant 3 The environment is *status quo, mediocrity*; the person is *compliant*. Quadrant 4 The environment is *micromanaged*; the person is *resistant*.

Creating a Culture of EMPOWERMENT and ACCOUNTABILITY

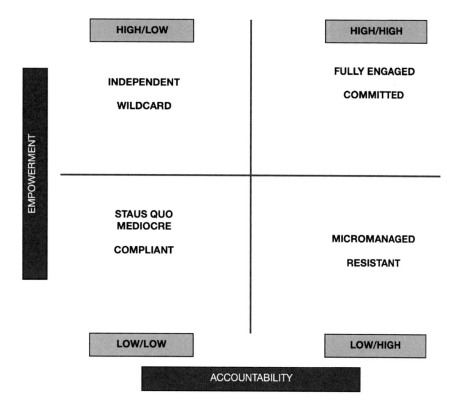

Empowerment

Empowerment calls for a culture of strong, visionary leadership that holds the organization's vision, mission and values or some form of statements to direct the purpose and fulfill the outcomes that are desired. This culture also recognizes the kinds of skills, abilities and outlooks that are needed to accomplish the desired outcomes. Clarity of expectations and communication is key to a healthy empowerment culture. Leadership requires emotional intelligence, knowledge, experience and wisdom. Specific abilities and skills required will vary with the purpose of the organization.

Empowerment and accountability cross over and complement each other in a healthy staff culture. I love to think of empowerment as helping others realize the very purpose they were created for in all their uniqueness. Empowerment without health accountability is weak and less than effective.

Accountability is the set up and the follow through that allows empowerment to be fully embraced.

In a recent cohort day with some second level leaders we took this matrix and they fleshed it out. Here are some of their brainstorming thoughts on the concept of empowerment:

- Appropriate supervision

- Engagement in mission

- Strength based

- Understand the why (the values)

- Clear feedback

- Can't treat as homogenized, or that means it cannot be an uniform approach

- Shared understanding

- Clear expectations

- Appropriate skill sets

- Right people—right job

This is one set of ideas that they came up with to describe an empowering culture from their perspective. Take the time with your team to flesh out the concepts that are important to you as a team.

Accountability

Accountability demands that clear roles, expectations and desired outcomes be provided. Each employee is given the opportunity to turn this into an accountability agreement that they take responsibility for. Then their supervisor revisits the accountability agreement with them for ongoing progress, stuck places and tweaks that may need to be made. Take some time to consider what an accountability agreement could help accomplish in your organization.

Columns one and three in the chart below give some information for understanding what an accountability agreement is in comparison to a job description. You will notice a blank column to note what your organization has in place.

Accountability Agreement	What is Your Focus?	Job Description
A strategic orientation towards the individual and the individual's role within the organization.		Considers neither goals nor strategic orientation of the individual.
Legitimizes and emphasizes a discussion of positive and negative consequences.		Consequences are exclusively in the employer's domain. They are not negotiable. Standard compensation package is primarily based on years of service and job level.
Based on multiple adult relationships.		Based on traditional parental orientation. The employer makes the rules.
Tailored to the individuals strengths.		Focused on the traditional definition of the job. The uniqueness of the individual does not measure in.
Takes a broad results oriented perspective.		Looks only at the job, it's tasks and activities. Generally ignores the outcomes for the clients.
Considers the big picture (all accountabilities) as well as the specific goals within a given time period.		The focus is on activities, competencies, past experience and formal education. No significance attached to goals or results.
Formal recognition that obligations and accountabilities appear at every level.		Does not generally consider accountabilities at any levels or in any direction.

Kaleidoscope Reflections

1. One way to create an opportunity to hear where your people are is to have them brainstorm what the desired environment, the people, thoughts, attitudes and behaviours would look like in each quadrant.

2. Define the words on the vertical and horizontal matrix. This is the base you will work from.

3. What word or concept would you use for each quadrant to describe:

    a. The environment—define what each descriptive word means.

    b. The employee or volunteer—define what each descriptive word means.

4. How could you create a tool for each leader to evaluate each employee/volunteer?

5. How could you create a tool for self-evaluation by employees/volunteers?

6. What would the principles of an accountability conversation be based on for evaluation and movement forward, whether it is inspirational or corrective?

7. How would the principles of an accountability agreement enhance each individual's ownership for being accountable for who they are and what they do for the organization?

8. What tensions would you see diminished by creating an understanding of what healthy empowerment and accountability looks like?

2. Productivity and Attitude Matrix

What-if your people understood that both productivity and attitude were two necessary principles for success and fulfillment both individually and corporately?

Often the measurement in a performance review is simply on the job getting done. And yet attitude is as powerful a measurement for suitability for the job as productivity is. If your people are engaged and focusing on being great in the role they were hired for, they are also culture influencers who enable the whole team to achieve outcomes and to let go of the drama.

Drama is an overreaction or exaggeration to an event that is out of proportion to the importance of that event. Drama usually exists in water cooler and parking lot conversations. These conversations rarely accomplish any positive movement forward. The focus is generally on the person rather than on the situation and its outcomes. Anytime the focus is on us, as we discussed in Section 1, it generally is about our ego needs.

As leaders we often feel the pressure to have the right answers on the tip of our tongues. There are times when stepping back and taking a moment of reflection gives us a much wiser and clearer answer that focuses our people in the right direction. Our stepping back also enables us to gain control of our reactions caused by our emotions. We can then turn those emotions into productive responses. Our raw emotions can at times give us clarity around a positive response and other times it can cause us to speak out of turn, or even make the situation worse than it needs to be. In leadership we have the opportunity to learn to use our emotions for positive energy. Our times of reflection are a great tool in helping us understand what sets us off and what we can do when we recognize that our emotions are leading us in the wrong direction even though it feels so right.

The following matrix I also used with a cohort of senior leaders to determine what they thought the behaviour would look like in each quadrant. See below the matrix for some of the brainstorming thinking.

Creating a Culture of Productivity and Great Attitudes

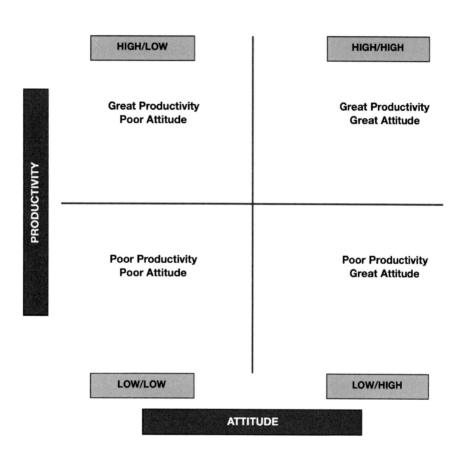

Here is a great team exercise. Take this same matrix and use the language that fits your people and your organization and create the descriptors you want to use.

Example:

Quadrant 1 High/Poor

The Lone Wolf—competent; superiority complex; rule driven; self-serving; job focus lapses in team orientation

Quadrant 2 High/Great

Role Model—self-motivated; motivates others; clarity of focus; alignment of mission; big picture perspective; inclusive communicators; leaders

Quadrant 3 Low/Poor

Team Killer—unmotivated; unproductive; negative; draining

Quadrant 4 Low/Great

Plant Waterers—love them; distracted; missing a skill; spinning wheel; may be teachable

 Kaleidoscope Reflections

1. Define the words on the vertical and horizontal matrix. This is the base you will work from.

   What word or concept would you use for each quadrant to describe:
   The environment—define what each descriptive word means
   The employee or volunteer—define what each descriptive word means

2. How could you create a tool for each leader to evaluate each employee/volunteer?

3. How could you create a tool for self-evaluation by employees/volunteers?

4. What would the principles of a conversation be based on for evaluation and movement forward whether it is inspirational or corrective?

5. How do you help people to move to where they can be and give their best? Look at each quadrant and at specific people.

6. What do you need to do to keep people where they can be and do their best?

There are tensions of all kinds as you lead. So often they are in the grey areas of leadership, which are not necessarily about right and wrong. Creating a matrix can aid in coming to helpful ways of navigating those tensions. In your first, or even second or third leadership roles, did anyone ever tell you to be prepared for tension? More often than not it was presented as conflict, which is true, and yet even the language of conflict over tension seems to have the potential to create a negative atmosphere.

I was a naive and wonder-filled leader when I started out. There were some great strengths found in that naivety and there were some great opportunities to end up in discouraging places. Naivety showed me to believe the best, as I wasn't aware that there could be anything less! Naivety also prevented me from seeing and grasping what was coming at me, whether good or bad. So I was unprepared for what was coming. I often felt pushed in a corner to have the right answer instead of the best possible answer for the situation. As a leader increasing in self-awareness, other awareness and taking the time to reflect, will lead to confidence and competence as you take bold action.

3. Change and Growth Chart

What-if we accepted change and growth as synonymous and therefore the tension they create is needed to move forward?

Volumes have been written on change and change management. I could not begin to top my favourite authors on change and transition: *Managing Transitions*; William Bridges, *Leadership on The Line*; Ronald A Heifetz, Marty Linsky.

The tension to consider here is the inner tension we all face whether it is expected or not.

In Section 1 Inspiration, we did extensive coverage of what inner conflict can do to us if we lack the ability to lead through it. In change, the challenge is to name what is really going on inside. What are the competing agendas we have, which we may not have identified and yet we find we have no peace to move forward? We set goals and wonder why they never get to a place of satisfactory completion. You may have set goals personally and/or professionally and find that you continue to have to backpedal. Or you may find that you get discouraged, as it seems you never quite get to where you want to be. The following exercise may be helpful to consider. It may give you aha moments and understanding in anything from weight loss, to leadership development, to life changing behaviours and goals.

Where Do You Get Stuck in Change?

All change is both technical or factual and adaptive or felt. As we consider change, we see that change takes all of us. Change is living in the in between. Consider the parts of the chart that follows.

Inner Change Resistant

Consider the points below and complete the assignments.	My Notes Change and growth are synonymous with each other. They both create pockets of resistance that is about our outlook and attitudes.
1. GROWTH POINT - name one for yourself. • Important area of growth for me? • Important area of growth for the team? EX. I want to learn to be more curious and softer in each conversation and situation rather than judgemental, directive and strident.	
2. BEHAVIOUR • What am I doing in this area of growth now? • What am I not doing? • Name how these behaviours are sabotaging my growth in this area? • Name why this new behaviour is important to you? Ex. I am letting my analysis become negative. I am creating stories through that negative sense which may not be true. **3. UNSPOKEN SABOTAGING THOUGHTS** • Name your fears and worries Ex. If I don't push this through, it will take too long and I might be perceived as being wrong • Name the tension of where you feel stuck in between the sabotaging thoughts and reality. Ex. I have to get this done, I must appear right and yet I need other input to truly be successful.	
4. TURN SABOTAGING THOUGHTS INTO PRACTICAL COMMITMENTS. • Create a What-If statement. Ex. What-if I 'STOP . REFLECT . RECALCULATE' and truly listen to the other person? What long term relational and beneficial gain will be developed? .	
5. DESCRIBE YOUR PLAN FOR MOVING FORWARD IN THIS AREA. EX. Pay attention to when I feel the sense of urgency in my gut and cost to stop, hit pause and learn to ask the curious question so we can bring the best of our ideas together for th egreater good.	

1. **Intuition**—our *gut* reaction—the question is, "What do I sense in this change?"

2. **Emotions**—our *heart* reaction—the question is, "What do I feel in and about this change?"

3. **Facts**—our *head* reaction—the question is, "What am I thinking in and about this change?"

4. **Behaviour**—our *hands and feet* reaction—the question is, "What am I doing and where am I going as a result of this change?"

 Kaleidoscope Reflections:

1. Describe a recent or current change.

2. When you consider the chart above, where would you say you tend to get stuck?

3. Explore what lies behind that sense of being stuck and what shifts in your thinking and attitude need to happen in order to move forward with the change?

4. When we look at change and have a sense of being stuck, there are times we look at outside sources of being stuck. The chart helps us look at what is really going on inside us. **What-if** we are stuck on the inside and sabotaging our own dreams? Take the time to work though the chart to uncover your inner resistance to the change you are facing. This makes a great team exercise in preparing others to work through their own change resistance.

Tensions are what keep us on our toes, what frustrate us beyond measure and are always with us. Learning the tools to navigate the tensions that come our way will enable us to lead with authenticity, strength and integrity for the greater good. It is a humbling and rewarding journey. Take the time to see tensions as a valuable resource and motivator for innovation, creativity, fulfillment and movement into the future.

The above matrixes express only two types of tensions we face as we seek to invest in others. Earlier we saw this continuum that a dear colleague, Greg, wisely shared, as a tension we face all the time. On a continuum place the word easy at one end and better at the other end.

Easy  Better

In the myriad of daily decisions that we make, we are constantly faced with the concept of, "Will I take the easy way which may work?" or "Will I take the better way which will have more far-reaching positive effects and probably will take more effort?"

 Kaleidoscope Reflections

A great team exercise is to give each person some sticky notes.

1. Have them take a few moments to jot one tension per sticky note that they face in their leadership roles.

2. Now have them give a story of how they experience that tension at work.

3. Have each one, share the tension and their story and turn this into a guided opportunity to help them think through the tension they are facing and to get to a clear thinking space to be able to move forward.

Notes—record your most significant thoughts to reflect on and to begin bold action.

Chapter 20

What-if You're Not Finished Yet?

Any seasoned leader knows that finishing is an *-ing* word not an *-ed* word! It is ongoing. As you have worked through **What-if** Leadership Journal you will have come to new levels of understanding of what it means to be a leader, to understand leadership and to embrace leadership development in fresh ways. New worlds open up to us to grapple with, figure out and decide what we want to do with them. It is exciting, it is exhilarating, and it is also exhausting at times. Creating rhythms in your life and leadership is what will give you sustainability for the long haul.

Hindsight is a wonderful teacher, and it also creates a space where we tend to walk in *the curse of knowledge*. As you have read and worked through this handbook, now is the time to look back and remember where you started from. It is time to remember how far you have come and how long it has taken you to learn, to master, to fall down and to get up and try again. This will also create a healthy mindset. It allows you to share your journey and your expertise. This will allow you to recognize that those you influence and interact with may have some similarities in their journeys and they may also have had a very different journey. This is where teamwork and investing in others becomes challenging and yet a rich and fulfilling leadership journey.

You are not finished once you are hired for a role, or have taken time to build your leadership philosophy, or have developed a healthy leadership rhythm of life. Wherever you are on the leadership development continuum, you are to be a developer of leaders for the future, for sustainable work, for a stable foundation for future generations to build upon. This comes as you engage in what your leadership philosophy is, when you entrust that to others and empower them to become all that they can be.

There is a world to inspire to greater leadership wholeness, to analyze, to acquire for and to head into bold action on behalf of.

What-if you became all you were intended to be as a future focused, sustainable leader and had the foresight to move through the successes, the challenges, the interruptions to create a leadership development culture for all those who come within your leadership influence?

What-if our world became a better place not just from what you do yourself, but also from all that you pour into others to make space for them to become future focused, sustainable leaders who are pouring into others?

What-if you created the **What-if** you dream of accomplishing yourself and **What-if** that dream spilled out to enrich the lives of others that became an unending stream of sustainable leadership development?

I began this book with the story of the poignant challenge my friend Jayne was given to rethink her document in such a way that would make the Chair of the Executive Council a better leader. This **What-if** question produced a huge kaleidoscope shift in her thinking from critique to a new perspective in helping a leader succeed and in so doing change the course of the organization. Together, she and her mentor spent five hours brainstorming and meticulously crafting each word of a one page document that nudged the situation toward a focused and collaborative environment for the Chair to more firmly grasp the mantle of leadership and feel supported in doing so. Of course one letter wasn't the answer to everything. Nothing changed overnight. It took time, it took further forthright conversations. But instead of building a wall, the shift in tone and purpose allowed for a strong relationship to develop so that when the next even bigger hurdle arose, the leadership team moved forward with purpose and clarity that was unprecedented.

What situation is whirling in your heart and mind now? What story needs a new plot line? Reach within yourself and have the courage to take the bold action needed. Allow yourself to see the stunning beauty that comes with a slight kaleidoscope shift. It may be the most important question you ever ask:

What-if?

Notes—record your most significant thoughts to reflect on and to begin bold action.

References

Chapter 1

Lance Secretan, Inspire! What Great Leaders Do (New Jersey: John Wiley and Sons, Inc, 2004), Page xxxii.

Chapter 2

Peter Morgan, Stephen Daldry, Philip Martin, Julian Jarrod and Benjamin Caron. *The Crown*. Left Bank Pictures and Sony Television, 2016, //www.netflix.com/watch.

Dennis Baker, "READY, FIRE, AIM, The Initiative Concept for Leadership Abundance and Success" May 10. 2017, https://leaderinfluence.net/2017/05/10/ready-fire-aim-the-initiative-concept-for-leadership-abundance-and-success/.

John C. Maxwell, 2011. *Beyond Talent*. New York: Harper Collins Leadership, reprint, Page 24.

Hans Christian Anderson, "The Emperor's New Clothes," *Fairy Tales Told for Children*. First Collection. Third Booklet. (Eventyr, fortalte for Born. Forste Samling. Tredie Hefte.1837).

Ernest Hemingway, *The Sun Also Rises* (New York: Scribner's,1925).

Chapter 3

Richard Eckersley, "Getting to The Heart of The Matter; The West's Deepening Cultural Crisis," *The Futurist*; Nov/Dec 1993; 27, 6; ABI/INFORM Global Page 8.

Concepts of credit card and cheque book taken from a training with Dr Laura Belsten, President at CEO Partnerships - Coaching Executives and Organizations.

James Kouzes and Barry Z. Pozner, *The Leadership Challenge* (San Francisco: John Wiley and Sons, 2003) Page 48.

Ashok Contributor Group. 2012."12 Great Quotes from Gandhi on His Birthday." *Forbes*, October 12, 2012. https://www.forbes.com/sites/ashoka/2012/10/02/12-great-quotes-from-gandhi-on-his-birthday/#7ec01f1133d8.

Dr. Henry Cloud, *Integrity: The Courage to Meet the Demands of Reality* (New York: Harper Collins Publishers, 2006).

Chapter 4

Lisa Barrett, "*Mental Health, A New Understanding*" New York, Time Books, an imprint of Time Inc. Books, a division of Meredith Corporation. New York, NY, 2018.

Chapter 8

Frederick Buechner, *Secrets in the Dark: A Life in Sermons* (New York Harper Collins Publisher, 2006).

Chapter 9

Michael Strahan Quotes. BrainyQuote.com, BrainyMedia Inc, 2019. https://www.brainyquote.com/quotes/michael_strahan_644475, accessed October 3, 2019.

Merriam Webster, s.v., "capacity(n)", accessed October 3, 2009, https://www.merriam-webster.com/dictionary/capacity.

Chapter 10

Joseph Meyers, *The Search to Belong: Rethinking Intimacy, Community, and Small Groups* (Grand Rapids: Zondervan, 2003) Page 41, 45-48.

Philip Blumstein, "The Production of Selves in Personal Relationships," in *The Production of Reality: Essays and Readings on Social Interaction*, 3rd ed. (Thousand Oaks: Pine Forge Press. 2001) Page 299.

Joseph Meyers, *The Search To Belong: Rethinking Intimacy, Community, and Small Groups* (Grand Rapids: Zondervan, 2003) Page 41, 45-48.

Ron A. James Heifetz and Marty Linsky, *Leadership on the Line* (Boston: Harvard Business School of Publishing, 2002) Page 199.

Chapter 14

Frederick Buechner, *Wishful Thinking: A Theological ABC* (New York: Harper Collins, 1993).

Chapter 15

Oxford Dictionary, s.v. "transformation(n)",accessed October 3, 2019, https://www.lexico.com/en/definition/transformation.

Stephen Covey, *The 8th Principle* (New York, Free Press, 2008) Page 49 -50.

Chapter 20

Peter Urs Bender, *Leadership from Within* (Toronto, Stoddart Publishing Company,1997) Page 42

Chapter 21

Marianne Williamson, *A Return to Love; Reflections on the Principle of a Course in Miracles.* (New York, Harper Collins, 1992)

Resource Page

1. **Values Inspired Living Cards**
   51 Values cards and their definitions to accompany the Values Exercise in Section I Inspiration.

2. **Notes to Inspire A 6 ½ x 10 notebook**
   A lined journal for recording your reflections and bold action.

3. **What-if Leadership Journal small 5 x 7 notebook**
   A simple lined notebook for taking notes.

All products available by going to RuthEsau.com. Check the Resources box and submit the contact form. You will receive a response within 24 hours.

Suggested Reading List

The following book list represents a small portion of the influencers, through written word, that have been a part of my life transforming journey. Each book has been blended with my beliefs, inspired my life and leadership and become a part of who I am and what I do.

1. *A Work of Heart*, Reggie McNeil

2. *Anatomy of Peace*, Arbinger Institute

3. *The Search to Belong*, Joseph Meyers

4. *The Making of a Leader*, Robert Clinton

5. *Integrity*, Henry Cloud

6. *Emotionally Healthy Spirituality*, Peter Scazzaro

7. *Inspire*, Lance Secretan

8. *Speed of Trust*, Stephen RM Covey

9. *The Leader's Journey*; Herrington, Creech, Taylor

10. *Leadership from Within*, Peter Urs Bender

11. *Becoming a Resonate Leader*, Annie McKee, Richard Boyatzis, Frances Johnston

12. *How to Think Like Leonardo DaVinci*, Michael J. Gelb

13. *The Courageous Follower*, Ira Chaliff

14. *Reality Based Leadership*, Cy Wakeman

15. *EGO*, Cy Wakeman

16. *Leadership and Self Deception*, Arbinger Institute

17. *The Leadership Challenge*, James Kouzes and Barry Z. Pozner

18. *Leadership on the Line*, Ronald Heifetze, Marty Linsky

19. *Fierce Conversations*, Susan Scott

20. *Leadership Sustainability*, Dave Ulrich, Norm Smallwood

21. *Boards That Lead*; Ram Charan, Dennis Carey, Michael Useem

22. *Governance as Leadership*, Chait, Richard P.

23. *Servant Empowered Leadership*, Don Page

24. *God in My Everything*, Ken Shigematsu

25. *Crafting a Rule of Life*, Stephen Macchia

26. *Necessary Endings*, Dr Henry Cloud

27. *A Beautiful Constraint,* Adam Morgan, Mark Garden

28. *Co-creative Coaching*, Laura Whitworth, Karen Kimsey-House, Henry Kimsey-House, Phillip Sandahl

29. *Immunity to Change*, Robert Kegan

30 *Getting to Maybe*, Frances Westly, Brenda Zimmerman, Michael Quinn Patton

31. *The Mentor's Mentor*, Corey Olynik

32. *The Practice of Adaptive Leadership*, Ronald Heifetz, Alexander Grashow, Marty Linsky

About The Author

Ruth Esau is an inspiring, outcomes focused leadership development author, speaker, facilitator and coach. Ruth is founder and president of Inspired to Lead and RuthEsau.com. Ruth and her husband, Brian of 47 years are blessed to have Melodie; Joy and Stacy, Brianna and Rebekah; Rob and Jasmine as their family.

Made in the USA
Middletown, DE
19 November 2019